Secrets of
Personal Command Power

Also by the Author

How to Make Ten Thousand Dollars a Year from "Lost" Sales. 1976. Parker Publishing Company.

Lloyd Purves on Closing Sales. 1978. Parker Publishing Company.

SECRETS OF PERSONAL COMMAND POWER

Lloyd Purves

Parker Publishing Company, Inc.
West Nyack, New York

© 1981, *by*

PARKER PUBLISHING COMPANY, INC.
West Nyack, N.Y.

Library of Congress Cataloging in Publication Data

Purves, Lloyd,
    The secrets of personal command power.

    Includes index.
    1. Success. 2. Control (Psychology) 3. Leader-
ship. I. Title.
BF637.S8P87   158'.1   80–21298
ISBN 0–13–798116–3

Printed in the United States of America

What This Book Will Do for You

This book is written in plain, understandable language to show you how to discover and use your personal command power. With this magical power you can attain heights you never thought possible; you can accomplish more than you ever dreamed. As you put the power secrets in this book to work, you can gain recognition, make more money, and win the success you want.

Through my years of experience in management, sales training, seminar conducting, public speaking, instructing and working with people from all walks of life, I have learned one striking fact: people want power. This is entirely commendable and wholly justified, since without power, life drags along, ambition wanes, and human resources wither and dissipate.

Yet, most people have more than enough power to run their lives effectively and successfully. The problem is that they have never learned to develop and use the personal command power that they already possess. Indeed, many do not even realize that they have this great well-spring of power; they cannot accept the reality of the power that can be theirs. It is a tragic personal loss that need never happen to you.

Personal command power is not vague and hazy, nor is it a passing fad. Rather, it is the inner strength which can be developed into a mighty force capable of taking you where you want to go. Personal command power is not fluffy mysticism: it is applied, personal logic—hard as rock and strong as steel.

This book is designed to tell you the secrets of personal command power. It shows how to get what you want without a fight; you will see that you do not have to compromise your ethics or abandon your common sense to be a winner if you use personal command power.

There is a wealth of exciting case histories in this book which will prove to you the miraculous results of personal command power. You will read:

- In Chapter 1, how Fred Walker turned his company around financially with control psychology.
- In Chapter 3, how John Walters struck pay dirt in the "strike zone" and won a choice teaching position.
- In Chapter 4, how Dr. S. A. Pritchford multiplied his personal command power using other people, and thus doubled the size of a hospital.
- In Chapter 6, how Sandy Reed infused her personal command power with enthusiasm and won a promotion, plus two proposals of marriage.
- In Chapter 7, about how realtor Jim Tillman quickly landed his biggest deal by using personal command power to make a strong first impression.
- In Chapter 14, how I used personal command power to lick my fear of public speaking.
- In Chapter 15, what happened when Don Perkins dropped his "Mr. Sugar" role and put personal command power to work.

These and dozens of other real-life examples will show you how to make the most of your own considerable personal command power. You will be surprised at the dramatic and gratifying results you can bring about through the powerful secrets in this book.

Most surprising of all is this: you will find that you do not have to climb over "dead bodies" to get what you want when using personal command power. This book shows that you can be a winner without being obnoxious, arrogant, or destructive. In fact, with personal command power, you can make friends who will be eager to help you achieve.

When you have mastered the secrets of personal command power you will be able to:

- Reach your business and personal goals.
- Make friends easily.
- Be better liked.
- Gain financial independence.
- Feel better about yourself.
- Look forward to each new day.
- Handle tough business assignments.
- Be a leader.
- Speak effectively and forcefully.
- Sharpen your management skills.
- Be justifiably proud.
- Be more helpful to your associates.
- Enjoy your family and friends.
- Gain recognition.
- Have prestige.
- Earn success.
- Be enthusiastic.
- Impress people.
- Be more self-confident.
- Get and keep whatever you want.

Personal command power can be yours when you have read and studied the many exciting chapters in this book. Personal command power is a vital, potent force. It is strong stuff. The power secrets in this book can put you in charge, beginning today!

Lloyd Purves

Contents

Contents

1

The Control Psychology
Secrets of
Personal Command Power

Control psychology is a key aspect of personal command power. As such, it behooves us to define, examine, and study this vital power element along with command power, which is the central theme of this book. Control psychology will be the chief tool you will be using to establish and enlarge upon your personal command power.

Control is the authority to guide, direct and manage. *Psychology* is the science of mind and behavior. Control psychology consists of the techniques and methods you will use to influence, guide, direct, and manage other people. It is the control that you will exercise over their minds and their behavior.

To command means to exercise a dominating influence over, or demand something as one's just reward. Power is the possession of control, authority, or strong influence over others. Since control psychology is a main element in command power, you must give it your close attention. You will see that it is woven through all the other power secrets that will be revealed to you in this book.

R. L. Turner, a bright young man with a marketing degree and five years' experience as a road salesman, had been handed the tough assignment of revitalizing a fragmented sales force. Due to the illness and advanced age of the retiring sales manager, a surly salesman with a short fuse named Wilbur "Willie" O'Neill had dominated the sales force. His ideas and methods ran counter to Turner's. At his first sales meeting, Turner stood grimly silent before the group, squarely in front of Willie O'Neill. Without moving his eyes from Willie, he began. "Gentlemen," he said, "I'm the sales manager and I am going to fulfill that responsibility. I expect full cooperation from each of you. Unless you are prepared to give that cooperation, now is the time to leave."

Turner moved to the front of the room. "Are there any questions?" he asked.

There was not one.

"Good," Turner said. "Now we will get down to business."

That was the year the sales team brought in a 25% increase, and R. L. Turner's concept of control psychology was the determining factor. In using control psychology to get what he wanted, not only had Turner benefited, but so had every salesman, the company, and the firm's customers. Control psychology has a domino effect. When you put it to work, the results and benefits keep piling up.

Marshall Goodwin had been sent by his firm, a manufacturer of electronic equipment, to address and explain the merits and applications of the company's products to a newly appointed sales agency. As twenty-seven year old Marshall stood before the group of veteran salesmen, he sensed that they were equating his competence with his years. Goodwin then put his control psychology to work in his opening remark. "I realize," he said, "that there are salesmen who know more about this product-line than I do. However, I see none of them present. So let's start at the beginning."

A few backs stiffened momentarily, but Marshall had put himself on a firm footing with a skilled bit of control psychology. Your command power has a solid basis when it is launched using control psychology. Furthermore—this power maneuver saves time and erases any doubts about who is in charge.

Bobbie Gailbraith, a hard-working secretary in the insurance firm of Walker and Turnbow, eliminated a problem with Vickie Summers by employing an abrupt and determined display of control psychology. Vickie wasted time during the day by talking on the phone, doing her nails, and engaging in other unnecessary personal matters. Then at 4:30 P.M., she would rush over and lay a pile of unfinished correspondence on Bobbie's desk. This went on for two weeks. Finally, the next Monday, when Vickie dumped her neglected work on Bobbie's desk, Bobbie picked up the unfinished letters, walked over to Vickie, held the letters high above Vickie's waste basket and dropped them in. The flustered Vickie sputtered for a few minutes, but she did get the idea.

Yet control psychology takes many forms; it does not always have to be abrasive.

For example, Clarence "Whitey" Crompton used his control psychology by feeding a purchasing agent's ego. Whitey recognized Fred Wetter's insecurity, so he clothed his control psychology in flattery laced around fragments of truth about Fred's personality. As a result, he gained an inordinate portion of business from the firm where Fred worked.

No matter what form it takes, control psychology must be used resolutely. Like all strong personalities, Whitey Crompton did not restrict his control-psychology techniques. He could apply it until it hurt, and his method was to select the most effective technique for the occasion. Employing objective analysis gives control psychology added impetus.

Kay Emerson raised money without her husband's help, and bought a gift shop. She was competent and her business thrived, while her less ambitious husband practically abandoned his insurance business to hang around Kay's place and offer little goodies of advice. Despite Kay's objections, he persisted in this behavior. Then one night he came home and couldn't get in the front or back doors. In a huff and panicking, he rushed back to Kay's shop where she was working late. He demanded to know why he couldn't get into the house. "I changed the locks," Kay stated. "When you decide to go back to work and run your business, I'll get you a key. I'll go home and give you your bags for now. A husband I want; a parasite I don't need."

Harsh words, yes. Control psychology, yes. It worked.

Now Kay and her husband compete on friendly terms to see who can run the best business enterprise. Control psychology is designed to do just that—control!

Jim Altman sells the most expensive automobiles made. He does it by using control psychology to influence and direct the prospect's mind. The gist of his technique is apparent when he says, "I have cheaper cars to sell, but I would be remiss if I showed one to a man of your position, Mr. Prospect. You can't afford anything less than the best."

Control psychology can be used to manipulate an individual's thought processes to your advantage. This puts people in a frame of mind to give you whatever you want.

Willene North is one of a growing number of female professionals. As a travelling auditor, she often eats alone in restaurants. When a hostess or maitre d' is hesitant about giving her a desirable table, she asks, "Are you interested in intimidating me, or will you give me a good table, now?" The results are electrifying.

Control psychology works in every situation and in all areas of personal and professional life. You can adapt it to your circumstances and move up from there. This is one of the valuable secrets employed in developing your personal command power (PCP).

HOW TO GRAB AND KEEP THE UPPER HAND

Control psychology is at work every hour of every day. You either use it to your advantage, or somebody else will be applying his own brand of control psychology on you! Grabbing and keeping the upper hand is the first step in making control psychology work for you. You can shock, soothe, cajole, bombard, dominate, persuade, insist, influence or manage as you grab control. You are the one who must choose the strategy and the ammunition as you seize the upper hand.

Keith Dodson was feeling depressed as he read the "Help Wanted" ads in the morning paper. He had been bumped from his railroad job by an older man who had insisted that his seniority be recognized. Although Keith had never sold anything, he noticed an ad asking ambitious salesmen to call a Mr.

Jarbo at a local hotel. Keith was bright enough to know that it was up to him to take charge, so he put control psychology to work. He dialed the number and said, "Mr. Jarbo, this is Keith Dodson. I'm your man and I'm on my way to see you right now."

There's more to the story, of course. The point is that Keith grabbed the upper hand by exercising control psychology. He got the job and did so well that he couldn't afford to return to his old place on the railroad when he was called back six months later. Grabbing the ball gives you the upper hand. With control psychology, you don't have to take just anything that comes along.

Once you have grabbed the upper hand, there is no time to coast. Keeping the upper hand demands a persistent use of control psychology.

Dennis Edwards had been transferred to an eastern city by his firm which dealt in securities and commodities. The men previously responsible for sales and clients sat around the office all day and drank huge quantities of coffee. That is, until Dennis took control. Out of five men, one, Mr. Seevers, rebelled: he still wanted to coast until noon. Dennis called him into his office. What happened follows.

Dennis: "Mr. Seevers, I respect your age and experience. One month ago, I established some rules about loafing in this office. Have you forgotten?"

Mr. Seevers: "No."

Dennis: "Good. You know what I am talking about then. There can be no exceptions. As long as I'm here, this office will be run on my terms. When you become the manager, you can run it as you see fit. Fair enough?"

Mr. Seevers nodded his head and got up and went to work. In all fairness, he produced his share of business from that point on. He was no fool; he now understood that the new boss who had grabbed the upper hand meant to keep it.

Now, let's ask a question. Who would really have been running that office if Dennis Edwards had relaxed after grabbing the ball on his arrival? Control psychology will enable *you* to grab the upper hand; it is the secret power that will keep you in charge.

WHAT TO DO WHEN YOU TAKE CHARGE
WITH CONTROL PSYCHOLOGY

What you do after you establish your authority is just as significant as taking charge in the first place. There is not much gain in grabbing the upper hand unless some thought has been given to what comes next. The following are some ideas that you can use to keep your PCP in action after you have taken over through using the secret of control psychology.

- Be single-minded.
- Refuse to be side-tracked.
- Don't be swayed by criticism.
- Hang in.

Being single-minded does not mean you should be narrow-minded. It means that once you have taken charge with control psychology, you must stay with your project. Any leader will tell you that his authority to control is challenged daily. When you are on top, be as single-minded as a blow torch. This will protect what you have won and will henceforth maintain your authority.

Steve Hamilton won a position as regional marketing director over a five-state area. Then his boss, M. D. Banks, called him in at the end of three months to tell him that he was being re-assigned to his old territory as a regular salesman. When Steve demanded to know why, Mr. Banks replied, "Steve, you were a strong salesman. You worked night and day to get that job as a regional director. As soon as you got it, though, you acted as if you only wanted to be one of the boys. You lost control and with it you lost the job. I'm sorry."

It's obvious that Steve neglected to single-mindedly give his attention to maintaining what he had worked so hard to win. Had he continued to apply control psychology after he had gained his primary objective, he would still be the boss. Control psychology is for keeping control as well as getting it.

Refusing to be side-tracked is an exercise in personal discipline. It is control psychology, self-applied, that works from the minute you make up your mind to get what you want, until you have it and more. Refusing to be side-tracked is the way to take full advantage of control psychology.

The more you win with control psychology, the more you will be criticized. This is the lot of the winner. The same control psychology that put you up front will dictate that you should not be swayed by disapproval. Take criticism for what it is worth. And often that is not very much.

Hanging in, of course, is persisting. You hang in to win. You hang in to stay a winner after control psychology secrets have put you in charge.

HOW FRED WALKER USED CONTROL PSYCHOLOGY TO TURN HIS COMPANY AROUND

Fred Walker was the comptroller of a medium-sized manufacturing company which had been a moneymaker for years. However, now the company was floundering: its cash-flow was weak, advertising had been curtailed, and sales activities had been slowed by drastic economic restrictions. In short, the whole structure was threatened with disaster.

Charles Swenson, president and major stockholder, on the advice of his chief operating officer, had brought in a high-priced consulting firm. The chief operating officer, himself an outsider, had recently been lured away from a competitor, and his credentials were impeccable.

Nevertheless, Fred was suspicious. He was disturbed that more and more of the company's money was going to the consultants, while the company's position steadily deteriorated. Fred had voiced his concern to Mr. Swenson, but he had brushed aside any suggestion that the consulting firm might be at fault. After all, the chief operating officer himself had arranged for the services of this firm.

Fred now put his control-psychology power to work: he was determined to gain control of the situation and save his company as well as his job. So he visited an officer in Mr. Swenson's bank, gained his confidence, and asked the banker to obtain a list of the consulting firm's officers. Guess who was high on the corporate list? Mr. Swenson's chief operating officer! There he was, enjoying a big slice of the juicy fees that the consulting firm was extracting from Fred's company.

The next morning, Fred walked into Mr. Swenson's office unannounced. He put his control psychology on the line. Holding up one hand to quiet Mr. Swenson, he laid the list of the consulting firm's officers before him, saying "Here is the first thing you ought to look at today." With that he turned on his heel and went back out the door.

Within twenty-four hours the chief operating officer was out on his ear. One month later, Fred was made a vice-president.

As you can see, the control-psychology element of PCP gets things done in high places. Yet it is equally effective in the more mundane areas of human activity. This creative force is your own personal property.

YOU CAN GET WHAT YOU WANT AND STILL KEEP ALL YOUR TEETH

Let's face it. There is such a thing as paying too big a price for something. You pay too much if you win the upper hand but later lose a mouthful of teeth when the strategy backfires. However, you can use control psychology to get what you want and still keep all your teeth. Some positive points will show you how to bring about the results you want without undue pain.

- Avoid humiliating your opponent when you apply control psychology. But, if the situation is such that somebody must suffer, don't let the rug be jerked out from under you. Go ahead and make your power play using control psychology. Then you can do whatever is necessary to keep the fire from spreading.

- When you are compelled to trample someone in order to get what you want, leave the way open for him to save face. You can be sweet to a competitor, or whoever stands in your way, even as you boot him aside. Let him save face, then he won't feel an overpowering urge to deprive you of your molars if he ever gets the chance.

- Be objective. This means dealing with the facts and realities of a situation without letting your emotions distort your good judgment. This is not to suggest that you should stifle your enthusiasm for getting what you want, but it does mean that logic is an integral part of control psychology.
- Don't get too much advice. Making up your own mind is the beginning of control psychology.
- Maintain your dignity. If you lose self-control, you lose *all* control. And possibly a few teeth.

Consider this, too: the only people likely to accept abuse, humiliation and embarrassment are poor, weak prospects who will have little to offer you. Powerful people deal with and motivate capable people. This is where your control psychology will be effective and profitable.

A final note on this subject. We have all read and heard of somebody who has moved heaven and earth with tactics bordering on the criminal. What we don't hear about is the aftermath of bloody noses, ill-feelings and the ultimate failure of such brutish philosophy.

Don't misunderstand. Control psychology is strong stuff. You don't have to apply it with a power puff. You can lay it on with fire and thunder if you mix a modicum of diplomacy with it. And you *can* keep your teeth as you apply the squeeze.

HOW TO AVOID SIGNS OF WAVERING

Nothing will undermine the force of control psychology more quickly than a hint of wavering or indecision. Any shakiness that indicates self-doubt makes it mighty tough to convince anyone that he is face to face with a strong-willed character.

To avoid any hint of wavering as you apply control psychology, map your strategy ahead of time. Stick with your plan. Don't be side-tracked by resistance, or unexpected last-minute developments. Being distracted or changing strategies can create problems which you can avoid with practice.

Granted, practice can be tedious. It often is for me, but I still do it because control psychology experts convinced me long ago that it is the best way to stay razor-sharp.

For instance, at a Chicago convention not long ago, I was going to join an audience of two thousand to hear an address by a nationally recognized human-relations expert who always mesmerized his audiences. As I came in by a side door, I saw this powerful man alone behind the stage curtain. He was practicing his presentation with all the fervor of a college debater, despite the fact that he had made this same presentation before in a dozen cities, before countless groups.

Do as the experts do. Practice what you plan to do and say. Practice aloud. Go through the whole routine, gestures and all. Practice—practice—practice. It is a proven way to eliminate any signs of wavering as you pour on the power with control psychology.

THE SECRET OF A STRONG FRONT

One of the keys of vigorous control psychology is the added power of a strong front because control psychology never creeps in by the back door.

Dean Robbins was a young professional, new in town and short of money. For business reasons, it was important to him to join an elite social club in his community, so he managed to arrange a meeting with the membership committee. He learned that old Leonard Cox ran the show, and on the appointed night, Dean strained his budget and rented a chauffered limousine. He called Mr. Cox and offered to pick him up and take him to the meeting, which impressed Mr. Cox. The added power of a strong front catapulted Dean right into the middle of the club's activities. Today Dean is vice-president of the club, and Mr. Cox is one of Dean's loyal business clients.

The secret power of a strong front is that it generates a favorable atmosphere in which to apply control psychology. With this added psychological advantage, you can take charge in a hurry.

SECRET TECHNIQUES TO MAINTAIN CONTROL

When you take charge with control psychology, you can anticipate opposition. By its nature, control psychology stirs up competition and a certain amount of opposition. This is no cause for alarm, but since some opposition is inevitable, it is better to be prepared for it. You are then in a position to keep the control that you establish with a psychological maneuver.

You can expect three types of opposition when you put control psychology to work. When you recognize the nature of the opposition that you are likely to face, you can then handle it and maintain control. The three basic types of opposition you may encounter are:

1. Open opposition
2. Hidden opposition
3. Ego-related opposition

Open opposition is easy to recognize. It's right there blowing up in your face. In this situation, you have a great advantage however, because you can use control psychology to deal with it. Deflate your opponent's charge by appearing to attach much less significance to it than he does. Keep your composure. Hang onto whatever you have won, while soothing him with reassurances that you are not indulging in a vendetta against him. Keep your voice steady and tolerant, and after he has blown off a head of steam, let him walk away with some of his self-respect intact. Meanwhile, you haven't sacrificed a thing.

Hidden opposition is a little harder to deal with since it most often takes place behind your back, in the shape of rumors, insinuations, gossip, and other insidious ploys. The secret is to root out and identify the opposition. Once it is uncovered, you can neutralize it with the same techniques you use to control open opposition. Don't dignify it by attaching undue importance to it.

Ego-related opposition can get to be a hassle. When your control psychology has won what you want despite the spirited opposition of some proud rival, you are going to hear from him.

Ego-related opposition is acute opposition. But it can burn out in a hurry, and will succumb to the same control-psychology secrets and techniques that will whip other forms of opposition.

Ned Sartain has a simple technique for dealing with opposition. As his opponent spouts off, Ned will say, "I know you believe what you are saying, but that can't change anything." He will vary this with, "I know how you feel, but I can't do what you ask." He repeats these power statements at appropriate intervals as he listens to the opposition's objections. Invariably, the opposition will cool down and back off.

Ned regards opposition as just another opportunity to prove his PCP by another exercise of control psychology. This is a winner's attitude.

INSTANT POWER POINTERS

- Control psychology is a key aspect of personal command power.
- Grabbing and keeping the upper hand is the first step in control psychology.
- What you do when you take charge with control psychology determines the final outcome.
- Personal control psychology is effective in high places as well as low places.
- You can get what you want with control psychology and still keep all your teeth.
- Practice eliminating any signs of wavering as you apply control psychology.
- A strong front creates a favorable atmosphere for control psychology.
- Opposition represents an opportunity to prove the power of control-psychology techniques.

2

How to Use
Personal Command Power
to Gain the Offensive

To gain the offensive means to attack: it means being the aggressor. When you have mastered the techniques and methods of using your personal command power to gain the offensive, you will have a big advantage because the very act of attacking puts you out front. When you take the offensive, you automatically and instantly establish authority, stabilize your direction, show determination and command attention and respect. Knowing how to use PCP to gain the offensive is a prized secret, so study it closely.

WHY STRIKING THE FIRST BLOW COUNTS THE MOST

The advantages of striking the first blow are impressive. The following list shows a few you will gain when you get in the first lick. Look it over and add some of your own.

- Takes the adversary by surprise.
- Promptly establishes your authority.

- Makes you the aggressor.
- Throws your opponent for a loss.
- Startles your competition.
- Gains extra time for you.
- Proves that you mean business.
- Discourages attacks against you.
- Ignites your enthusiasm.
- Gives you a head start.

HOW TO USE SURPRISE TO GAIN THE OFFENSIVE

Surprise is an advantage long recognized by military leaders. Yet, it is equally effective in other fields. For example, Riley Houser was a small-town boy working his way through the ranks. His job was to help load trucks early in the morning at a giant wholesale grocery operation. Much of the merchandise was palletized and Riley operated a fork lift in the loading area. He really needed that job, but Bud Hale, his foreman, was foul-mouthed, big and abusive. Despite his tendency to be somewhat shy, Riley made up his mind to put a stop to Hale's senseless tyranny. The next Monday morning, he took the foreman by surprise. Before he mounted his fork lift, he walked up to Mr. Hale, stood squarely in his path and said firmly, "Mr. Hale, if you foul-mouth me one more time I'm going to climb off that fork lift and lay one right in your teeth."

Bud Hale blustered a bit, but Riley stood his ground.

The other warehouse employees have yet to account for the change in Bud Hale's manner. Riley Houser knows that it happened when he shook off his nagging feeling of inadequacy and got in the first lick to put a surprised brute in his place.

The first blow establishes your authority because it demonstrates your strength to move decisively. Riley Houser's case shows how this works. It took only one young man, striking one first blow, to establish the authority that ended a degrading situation for twenty warehouse employees. And it all came about without bloodshed. It pays to consider this option.

HOW TO HANDLE THE RISKS OF OFFENSIVE TACTICS

Of course, there is an element of risk involved in putting your command power to work. You may have some abrasive encounters, but ninety-nine times in a hundred, you can pour on the power without upsetting anybody. Command power does not automatically negate diplomacy and civil behavior; nevertheless, it is a mistake to back off when there is a risk of some unpleasantness.

Yes, there is a risk involved in being strong and assertive. But the risk is much greater if you ever hesitate to use your PCP. In this case, the risk is that you will be held back, trampled, and frustrated. This is no choice for the strong-willed and aggressive achiever.

Striking the first blow makes you the aggressor. This is a key point when you have a problem, since the whole affair often takes on an entirely different perspective when you are the aggressor.

This principle worked for Jack Sobin in a battle with an incompetent, scared credit manager. The man had been hired from outside the company, and apparently his former company's accounts receivable were far fewer than Jack's firm carried from month to month. In any event, one of the first things he did was to send a tactless letter to each account, reducing the open credit line and shortening terms from 2% for 30 days to 2% for 10 days. Customers and salesmen alike rebelled, but it was Jack who aggressively struck the first blow to remedy the situation. When Mr. Firestone, a partner in one of Jack's biggest accounts, complained vehemently to Jack, Jack aggressively took action. He dictated a scorching letter to the president of his firm, had Mr. Firestone's secretary type it on Firestone and Ambers letterhead, then took it in to Mr. Firestone, who was more than glad to sign it. Jack personally mailed the letter within the hour. The next week, the new credit manager rushed out another letter to the customers, this one rescinding the first, apologizing for the "misunderstanding," and pledging full cooperation between the customers and the sales force.

Jack had pulled off his aggressive maneuver by striking the first blow against a disastrous policy. He did it so smoothly that his opponent, the weak credit manager, never knew from where the lightning had originated. However it's dealt, the first blow has the greatest impact in firing up your PCP. As the aggressor, you have a potent, secret advantage that gives you a head start on whipping a problem or handling a bothersome opponent.

The first blow sets up your opponent for a loss: he is behind right from the start and he knows it. Witness how quickly Jack Sobin's unwitting opponent changed his tune when he was subjected to the first blow. This will work for you too when you need to strike the first blow in dealing with a tacky situation or stubborn foe.

Getting in the first lick startles your opponent. When you scatter the competition's thinking and surprise him with the first blow, you can take charge before he recovers.

Midge Evans, the newly-elected chairwoman of the Springfield Business Women's Club, was having a hard time with Jeanne Carrollton, who had also campaigned for the job. Jeanne had disrupted the first two weekly meetings Midge had conducted, so as Midge took the microphone to start the third meeting, she startled the troublemaker with a decisive first blow, settling the matter. She began with, "This is a professional club and I am the elected chairwoman. One member seems unable to grasp that. But from now on, we are going to have order and conduct our business in the time allotted. If there is any question about that, Miss Carrollton, let me explain that not only cooperation but courtesy is expected of each member." Jeanne was caught off guard by this unexpected blow, and before she could regain her composure, the meeting was over. As you can guess, Midge Evans has since been enjoying peace and quiet: she is in full charge, and doing the club a great service.

Once again, you can see how the first blow counts the most in gaining extra time for you. When you take the adversary by surprise, aggressively establish your authority, throw him for a loss, and startle him into submission, you have more time to go after what you want. This is reason enough to keep your PCP geared and ready to land the first blow.

ESTABLISHING AND BUILDING ON YOUR REPUTATION

Striking the first blow or making the first move proves without a doubt that you mean business. Any time you strike the first blow, you will be taken seriously. There are many psychological explanations for this, but it simply means that when you get in the first lick, everyone knows that you are determined to get what you want, accomplish your goal, and be a winner regardless of the obstacles.

Your reputation as a tough go-getter grows quickly when you perfect the command power technique of striking the first blow because this naturally discourages attacks against you and your ideas. Steve Hamilton, the top salesman for a diversified plastic packaging corporation used to sit back and wait for competition to hit him with wild prices and big promises, then he would counterattack. He lost a lot of sleep and considerable business until he made up his mind to strike first himself with hot prices and special promotions. Today he has the reputation of being a tough competitor and a smart operator, and, not surprisingly, his competition has cooled considerably. By striking the first blow, Steve put his competitors on the defensive, which discouraged attacks against him.

Two more advantages gained by striking the first blow are the ignition of your enthusiasm and the head start it gives you.

Nothing generates your own eagerness better than a winning strategy. When you strike the first blow, you see instant results which fire your enthusiasm to keep the pressure on, until the whole job is done. This exciting technique can always get your enthusiasm boiling as it gives extra zip to your PCP.

Striking the first blow gives you a head start, and the advantages of this in whipping any project into shape are so obvious that lengthy discussion here would be superfluous. As a driving, ambitious personality, you are not likely to overlook or neglect the power that comes from gaining the offensive and getting a head start.

HOW RICK MAJORS MADE AN EXTRA $2,000 BY STRIKING THE FIRST BLOW

There are many techniques to use in striking the first blow to gain the offensive. You don't often need a big stick. Just beating the competition to a juicy plum is one way to hand out the first jolt. Rick Majors gained the offensive by using this method and earned himself an extra $2,000 in the process.

Rick is a salesman for a large real estate and investment company whose firm had just listed an elegant house in the most prestigious part of town. The selling price was $500,000, and the house had to be sold within thirty days at the owner's insistence. This put considerable pressure on Rick Majors' company, and because of the abbreviated listing period, the president of the company offered a two thousand dollar bonus to the salesperson who sold the house. Most of the sales force seemed to take it for granted that Martin Blaine, senior salesman par excellence, would nab that prize money as usual. But instead, Rick Majors went on the offensive. While Martin Blaine was busily preparing an offer for an executive who was new in town, Rick went out the door with the listing sheet and a contract. Everybody knew about this wealthy new executive because the company president had tossed the name out at the sales meeting that morning. But only Rick had him in his car within the hour, looking at the $500,000 house. Two hours later, he had his sales contract signed and his bonus sewed up, simply because he beat super-salesman Martin Blaine to this red hot prospect.

Being there first can deal your opponents a devastating blow as you go on the offensive using PCP. Aggressive people like Rick Majors often use this technique: it is a winning maneuver.

HOW A FAST DECISION
GIVES YOU THE OFFENSIVE EDGE

Decision-making is not the most relaxing exercise in the world, but it is a prime tool for gaining the offensive.

We all know a few unfortunate individuals who squirm like a worm in hot ashes when they are faced with a decision. For those with little or no inner power, it is an excruciating demand. These unfortunate people find it difficult to answer a simple question straightforwardly. Obviously, people who can't or won't make decisions are running scared from the wrong thing at the wrong time and for the wrong reason. By contrast, the strong-willed man or woman uses decision-making to gain the edge. Two contrasting examples illustrate the point.

Case 1: A number of years ago, I watched the deterioration of a handsome, educated man, and the disintegration of a fine old corporation. Roger Safire, a successful mathematician and engineer, accepted the presidency of a company at the behest of a major stockholder who just happened to be his father-in-law. Roger, who could easily arrive at a decision based on a mathematical formula, found that dealing with people isn't that cut and dried. As the new president, he postponed, evaded, or ignored decisions that are vital to the health of any institution or individual. Able workers threw their hands up and found employment elsewhere, where leadership made the decisions. Roger's firm lost business, fell behind its competitors technologically, and gave up the rank it had enjoyed in the industry for so long. Yet Roger didn't even decide when to retire; he had to be forced to do so early. Today, the board of directors and a new president are still struggling to put together what had once been an empire.

The inability or refusal to make decisions is tragic. It erodes confidence, loses friends, and destroys power, as Roger Safire discovered.

Case 2: About the time Roger Safire's life and company were coming apart, I sat in a woman executive's office in Kansas

City and watched her make five important decisions in four minutes. She okayed the purchase of a truck, approved a new employee, ordered two carloads of potatoes, declined a dinner date, gave me the order I asked for and was on the phone before I could get out the door. This woman exuded power and it's small wonder her tracks were seen all over the Midwest. She took full advantage of the secret power of a fast decision which gains the edge and keeps the offensive.

There are two crucial points to be learned from these two cases. One, the time to make a decision is when the problem raises its head. This keeps you on the offensive and gives you the extra edge. Two, the wrong time to decide is later, when the options have vanished.

HOW TO MAKE A FAST DECISION
TO GAIN THE OFFENSIVE

How do you make a fast decision to gain the offensive? Some essentials include:

• Organizing the facts

When it comes to making a fast decision, you do not have time to go cherry-picking. Assemble only the facts that pertain to the decision you must make. All others are irrelevant for your purpose. Be objective, don't let your opinions or prejudices get in the way, look at the problem for what it is and consider only what needs to be done to bring about the results you want. The following is an example of these points.

Roy Casaday was put in charge of a large discount store's plumbing center, and buying was his responsibility. Roy knew and liked the store's current supplier who only had plumbing fixtures, but Roy wanted more. He disregarded the emotional tug that told him to stay with the old source, and instead called in Master Plumbers' Products, Inc. This company had bath fixtures, vanities, vanity tops, wall-surrounds, lavatories, toilets, bathtubs, showers, and more. They had a full merchandising program, full-color consumer product literature, well-illustrated installation manuals, promotional programs, and an enviable assortment of sales aids and displays, along with a mobile training center for instructing store personnel. Furthermore, Roy verified that Master Plumbers had an excellent performance record and a triple A financial rating. With all these verifiable facts, Roy made a quick decision. In this case, an objective exercise of his PCP brought about the desired results. The department leaped ahead when Roy went on the offensive with his quick decision, and Roy's income also gained—to the tune of five thousand dollars a year!

● Getting facts in a hurry

Obviously a fast decision does not permit unlimited time for research, so you must get your facts in a hurry.

● *Ask an authority.* An authority is an individual with experience involving special skills and special knowledge. Of course, the authority you seek must be one who is an expert in the area where you need quick help. Examples of authorities include:

Accountants
Lawyers
Doctors
Managers
Sales or marketing consultants
Bankers
Teachers
Tax consultants
Counselors

● *Reference books.* References such as technical books, sales books, text books, and a host of other fact-filled publications are available to you at public libraries, book stores, schools, and universities. These volumes and a good librarian can give you the needed facts in a hurry.

● *Personal observation.* Making a fast decision to gain the offensive is a personal undertaking. One secret of command power is keen personal perception. By observing carefully, you will uncover many facts and will speed up your offensive. Sharp eyes and keen ears are great offensive tools.

● Limiting your choice

When a decision is to be made, there is usually a multitude of choices available. Do not let this slow you down; instead, limit your choices, consider only the best two, weigh them quickly, and then drop the least effective. In reality, only one choice is needed. That is all you can afford to consider for more than two seconds.

● Accepting opinions for what they are worth

Don't ask for an avalanche of opinions before making a decision since free opinions are usually worth about what they cost. Wise counsel is, of course, sometimes advisable. But too much conversation will hinder a speedy decision, and too many opinions will slow down any offensive. You must make *your* own decision: your command power is at stake.

HOW TO KEEP ON THE OFFENSIVE

There is no such thing as reaching a plateau of personal power and coasting along for the rest of your life. PCP does not rest on assumptions. Once you develop the power you need and want, you must keep on the offensive to hang on to what you gained.

Larry Strube is a veteran independent insurance agent who has a clientele and an income that most of his competitors only dream about. Yet at age 54, Larry is still an aggressive salesman, constantly gaining new accounts while serving old clients. In a speech before the Underwriter's Club, he recently explained his simple philosophy: being a winner means constantly being on the offensive. Consequently, he is out in the field every day, and emphasizes that old friends vanish, skills grow dull, ambition wanes, and personal power erodes if you slack off. His sales record gives testimony to his words.

Two more authoritative power points will give breath and fire to your continuing offensive as you go after what you want:

- *Take nothing for granted.* Believe only what you know is true, not what you wish was. Watch for hidden motives as you deal with people and keep in mind that your goals are not all that important to your associates, co-workers, and friends. They may all wish you well, but they won't launch a long-range offensive on your behalf. However, don't let this fact make you distrustful or neurotic because good things do happen, and you will meet some helpful people. Just don't count on it. Rely on your own PCP to keep your offensive in high gear: that is a basic success secret.
- *Deal with people as they are.* This will maintain your offensive and keep your PCP boiling. It is noble to try and improve your fellow man, yet harsh reality shows that you do not have time for it. And if you did have the time, your chances of altering an opponent's personality or character would be remote indeed.

Edward Carlton, president of Carlton, Inc., a jewelry manufacturer, hired three young men, one after the other, and had to fire each of them. Each was bright and full of promise and Edward felt he could turn them into productive workers, although none of them had a record to justify Edward's optimism. On the fourth try, Edward employed a man with a commendable employment record and demonstrated ability who became a partner in Carlton, Inc. Edward now says only Santa Claus can be charitable in dealing with people.

Strong individuals intent on gaining the offensive must deal with people as they are. Changing people is difficult enough for the best psychiatrist; a busy man or woman bent on gaining the offensive certainly cannot afford this luxury.

INSTANT POWER POINTERS

- To gain the offensive means to attack.
- Taking the offensive establishes authority.
- The first blow counts the most.
- Surprise is an advantage.
- Striking the first blow proves that you mean business.

- A winning strategy generates personal enthusiasm.
- You get extra power with a head start.
- A fast decision gives you the offensive edge.
- The time to make a decision is when the problem raises its head.
- Too much conversation hinders a fast decision.
- You must keep on the offensive in order to retain what you have gained.
- Take nothing for granted.
- Deal with people as they are.

3

Secret Strategy: Aim
for the Strike Zone

The strike zone is the area, the time, the place, the subject and the person that can get the job done for you in the shortest time possible when you are exercising personal command power. It is the target you select and the immediate contact point you aim your power strategy toward for the greatest impact. This is your opponent's weak spot, where he is most vulnerable: it is the logical place to attack.

IDENTIFYING YOUR OPPONENT'S STRIKE ZONE

The first step in identifying the strike zone is to concentrate on your goal. If you feel guilty about going tooth and nail after what you want, you will be in trouble; somebody else will see your strike zone first and you may find yourself on the receiving end of an attack. Instead, find your opponent's weak spot and make the most of that strategic bit of knowledge.

FINDING OUT WHAT YOUR OPPONENT
IS AFRAID OF LOSING

The strike zone is often what the opponent fears losing most. When you aim for this target, you can win in a hurry.

Gary Metz, president of a modestly sized manufacturing plant, anticipated a large gas and electric bill each month. However, when his electricity bill jumped $1,000 per month although he had added no additional equipment and was operating for the same number of hours, he called City Utilities. Bob McHan, City Utilities' manager, claimed it was probably the computer's fault. But, at the end of three months, Metz's company was still being overcharged and Bob McHan was still making excuses. Finally Gary made one more call. He told McHan that he was taking his attorney and going to see the mayor in one week unless he had received credit for the overcharges. Gary was also very aware that McHan and the mayor had been having a running feud. Bob McHan protested, "I'll lose my job if you do that!"

"You have one week to save it," was Gary's reply.

Within three days, the credit was forthcoming and the error corrected. All this flurry of action was brought on only when Gary threatened his indifferent antagonist with the loss of his job—which was the one thing that insecure Mr. McHan feared losing most.

Even the meanest opponent has something he is afraid of losing. This is the strike zone you can use to your advantage, just as Gary Metz did, and with a bit of careful observation, you will soon uncover what your foe cherishes most and wants to keep. You probably won't have to take it away from him: just threatening to do so is usually enough to bring him to his senses. But if he proves obstinate, use your PCP for all you are worth by doing exactly what you promised the person you would do. Your PCP will help you win.

STRIKE ZONE: THE OPPONENT'S SUPERIOR

In many cases, an opponent's superior is the best possible strike zone, and he usually isn't hard to identify. Going over an opponent's head to turn him around may not be the only way to get results, but it is a highly effective method. When you identify and aim at this strike zone, something has to give, as the next example illustrates.

Jeff Hirsch, supermarket manager for a big grocery chain, caught Kirk Henry on two occasions delivering fewer loaves of bread than the store's invoices required. Both times Henry made flippant excuses. However, the third time, Jeff picked up the phone, and called the president of Old Colony Bakers, Inc. He explained his problem with the company's route salesman and told Marshall Goodwin, Old Colony's president, that one more such incident and both Old Colony Bakers *and* the route salesman would be out on their respective ears. Further, Hirsch threatened to give a full report to his headquarter's office.

The next morning, Marshall Goodwin was in Jeff's store before Kirk Henry's delivery time. When Henry came in, there was a 3-man conference and there hasn't been a hint of hanky-panky since. Henry is now a model of efficiency and courtesy since Hirsch unloaded a volley into his strike zone.

Going over his head may make it tough on the other guy; nevertheless, when he leaves you no choice, let him have both barrels right in the strike zone just as Jeff Hirsch did with his brilliant display of PCP.

STRIKE ZONE: MAKING THE OPPONENT AWARE

Merely letting a disagreeable oaf know that you have identified his strike zone is frequently more than enough to gain the desired effect. Clyde Norris, a soft-goods salesman, had to deal with a department store buyer who would see salesmen only on Wednesdays. However, Clyde knew no buyer for a concern as huge as Johann's, Inc. could do his job in only one day a week. So when Clyde arrived in town on a Monday and was told again by Jabuc's secretary that "Mr. Jabuc only takes appointments on Wednesdays," Clyde took aim at what he recognized as the strike zone. He instructed the secretary to ask Mr. Jabuc if the president of Johann's, Inc. was aware that one of his buyers worked only one day a week. She came back with the surprising news that Mr. Jabuc could "work Clyde in" at 11:30 that morning. The first order that Clyde got from Johann's wasn't world-shaking, but it opened the gates to a more cooperative relationship between the buyer and seller.

When somebody is throwing his weight around, let him know that you have identified his strike zone. The results will be startling.

STRIKE ZONE: OFTEN OBVIOUS

Strike zones are usually fairly obvious if you know anything at all about the obstinate troublemaker you are dealing with. The key is to hit the strike zone without delay. By striking a quick blow at an obvious strike zone, Irene Farmer got an $800 per year raise on the spot.

Irene had asked for a $50 a month raise, which was modest enough considering her work load as bookkeeper and receptionist in a one-woman office at Altman's Delivery Service. The second time she asked for the raise, Jim Altman suggested that they discuss it on a weekend trip together. Irene said, "Fine. Let's go discuss the trip and the raise with Mrs. Altman first." Altman threw his hands up and bellowed, "Okay! Okay! You've got your raise. Eight hundred. Okay? Okay?"

A strike zone can be as obvious as a jealous wife, or as obscure as a closet full of skeletons. Observe what concerns your opponent most, what he cherishes deeply, and what scares him most. Thus you will soon find and identify his strike zone. Then, don't waste precious time: take aim, and turn your PCP loose. You will get what you want, and your opponent will get a valuable lesson in power strategy.

THE SECRET OF HITTING
WHERE IT DOES THE MOST GOOD

The secret behind this concept is a simple one. Don't broadcast ahead of time what you are going to do. If you talk or brag too much, voice angry determination, or openly express hostility, you are going to stir up unnecessary resistance which will weaken your strategy. Brent Lincoln learned this principle the hard way.

Young Brent worked in the New York office of a large national concern. As part of their training, it was this company's policy to move young men of management caliber from one area of the country to another. Brent was transferred to a southern city where he came into direct conflict with his superior since Brent didn't think the old boy moved fast enough. It wasn't long before Brent had let everyone in the plant know that he was going to try and kick the old manager out. Unfortunately for Brent, the manager heard about Brent's plan and fired him. But Brent was lucky: the company appreciated his potential and didn't want to waste their investment in him, so they called him back to New York to teach him to keep his mouth shut. The irony of the situation was that his company had every intention of making him the manager of that plant and somebody else got the job because Brent blew it by giving his secret away. He had identified the company's trouble spot: the weak manager. He was Brent's strike zone, but his loose tongue and bit of bragging robbed him of his target.

For argument's sake, let us parallel Brent's behavior with that of his replacement, Mike Cooper. Mike quietly went to work with his eyes open and his mouth closed. He soon made several recommendations to his New York office, and the plant picked up momentum. At the right moment, Mike suggested that Bob Mason, the tired, aging manager, would really be happier coasting into retirement as an installation supervisor. The end result was exactly as Mike planned. Both men are now happy and competent in their new jobs, and to this day, only Mike knows how he worked on the strike zone. His secret strategy of hitting where it did the most good won him the job he wanted, without demoralizing the man who stood between him and his goal. This is ideal, but winning is still the name of the game where PCP is at stake.

HOW JOHN WALTERS WON
A CITY MANAGER'S POSITION

John Walters had returned to his home town where he was being interviewed for the position of City Manager. John was the best qualified of the candidates, having the academic credentials along with two years' experience as an assistant city manager elsewhere. John really wanted this job which would lead to bigger things, and in the meantime, he would be living and working in a town he loved. Unfortunately, he did have one problem: Melvin Ervine, councilman and industrialist, opposed him even though everybody else favored him and his obviously superior qualifications. Mr. Ervine, however, was trying to ease Gene Roper, an old crony, into the job despite his candidate's lack of experience and training, in a blatant attempt to repay a political debt.

John put his PCP to work: he went to a friend who worked at the local newspaper and together they dug through old files and did some in-depth research. They learned that Gene Roper had once lost his real estate license and had narrowly escaped going to prison. John's reporter friend also discovered that Mr. Ervine habitually squeezed kickbacks from his firm's suppliers as tax-free income. John Walters had found his strike zone and zeroed in for the kill.

The next day, he was in Ervine's office. "Mr. Ervine," he began, "Are you opposing my selection as city manager because I haven't offered you the kickback you extract from Cutter Plastic Supply and a few others I can name? And do you favor Gene Roper because he almost went to jail because of that real estate deal you involved him in a few years ago?"

Mr. Ervine was momentarily startled, but he was a cool one, and smilingly regained his composure. He assured John that, as a matter of fact, he had reconsidered and would approve his appointment. John, of course, accepted the position and his newspaper friend took care of the kickback matter. Often, when you find and hit the strike zone, the results exceed expectations.

WHY THE SHOT-GUN APPROACH WASTES POWER

Let this fact stick in your mind: the shot-gun approach, striking out in all directions and at everything, wastes power because it is a sure way to stir up needless resistance and bitterness. On the other hand, when you remember the secret strategy of aiming for the strike zone, you enhance your chances for quick success without wasting your energy. If you use the shot-gun approach, your power will be so fragmented it will lose much of its vitality and persuasiveness. Some forthcoming examples will spur you on.

Years ago, I learned the value of aiming directly and exclusively at the strike zone. I was coming up through the ranks of a large corporation which was having some accounting difficulties in a branch taken over by a new manager in a big Texas city. I was sent to take over the bookkeeping department until the branch could smooth out its wrinkles. Although bookkeeping was not exactly my cup of tea, my superior knew that I had some knowledge of that field; besides, travelling was an essential part of the company's training program. I soon found that straightening out the office procedure was easier than I had hoped, and I was soon using my spare time to call on customers the branch had lost or never contacted at all. Before long I had added twenty new accounts to a branch operation that sorely needed them.

One morning when I arrived early at the office, the phone was ringing. The caller was J. D. Phillips, our southern supervisor, who asked for Adrian Ponder, the branch manager. When I explained that Mr. Ponder wasn't in (I didn't say he was usually late), Mr. Phillips said, "Well, I'm sorry to miss him. I just wanted to call and congratulate him. He wrote me that you saved him so much time that he was able to go out and put on twenty new accounts. Will you convey my message to him?"

I said, "Yes, sir, I will." I didn't tell him that Ponder hadn't even left the office and would rather have taken a beating than call on a potential account.

When Ponder came in, I was duly armed: I had a message for him. I had my strike zone, and my sights were on dead center.

"Mr. Ponder," I said, "I have a message from Mr. Phillips for you. First, though, I have one of my own. Since my work has been so helpful to you, I want a ten dollar a week raise." (That was a lot of money in those days.) "And, I want your help in getting the sales manager's job in Texas when Ted Joiner retires the first of the year. Now, here's Mr. Phillips' message. He asked me to convey his congratulations to you for putting on those twenty new accounts all by yourself since I've been here."

Ponder may have been unethical, but he was no fool. He got the message loud and clear, and I got the raise and the new job. Remember: the strike zone is always the opponent's vulnerable spot.

HOW TOM HENNINGS COLLECTED

Tom Hennings had been sent by Marshtown Lumber and Supply Company to do a major remodeling job on Jim Sears' home, with Marshtown furnishing all materials and labor. In the agreement, Marshtown would pay Tom as soon as the job was completed, but after three months, Tom still hadn't been able to collect. Now he knew that he had to employ a stronger strategy since polite requests had been fruitless, and he was bright enough to know that Marshtown's customer was its vulnerable spot. He took aim at the strike zone and he wasted no time considering any other alternatives.

The next morning, he was knocking on Jim Sears' door. Tom explained that he had been unable to collect from Marshtown for the work he had done on the Sears' home.

"That's not my problem," snorted Mr. Sears. He changed his tone, however, when Tom calmly replied, "Well, maybe not, Mr. Sears. But much as I dislike it, I will be obliged to put a mechanics' lien on your house if the bill isn't paid in one week."

Tom wasn't absolutely sure he could do it, but nevertheless, his threat had the desired effect. Mr. Sears jumped straight up about three feet and yelled, "Why that dirty blankety-blank! Come on, I'll go with you. Let's get your money."

Thirty minutes later, the two men were in the office of Earl Shape, owner of Marshtown Lumber and Supply. Mr. Sears fumed, "Pay this man, you deadbeat, or I'll let everybody in town know how you operate!"

There were a few more heated exchanges, then Mr. Shape wrote a check for $2,500 and handed it to Tom Hennings.

So when you have a tough nut to crack, use the strategy that Tom Hennings put to work. Go for your opponent's vulnerable spot. If you have to stomp on a few toes, don't do it barefoot.

YOU CAN MULTIPLY YOUR PCP
BY CONCENTRATING

The strategy of aiming for the strike zone calls for intense personal control. Power always demands personal discipline, and concentration is the key: you can multiply your PCP by totally concentrating on your objective. As we know, the shotgun approach weakens PCP since such haphazard tactics denote confusion and indecision. But when you program your campaign with a generous dose of concentration, you multiply your PCP over and over. Nobody can hit the strike zone with a handful of confetti. The secret is to keep your mind on the number one objective until your primary goal is obtained. Then you can move on to secondary projects with order and authority.

June Perry used concentration to win a simple concession from her husband by refusing to be distracted or swayed.

June had her heart set on a thick outdoor "grass" carpet to go with her new patio furniture. However, her husband felt that a lighter weight would be preferable.

"But I want the heavy grade," June said.

"The heavier weight will hold more water and stay wet longer," her husband argued.

"You're right," conceded June. "But I want it."

"It will show definite footprints with that high pile," protested her husband.

"Yes," June replied, "but I want it."

"You'll get tired of it before it begins to wear out," her husband worried.

"Maybe so," agreed June. "But I want it."

"Well, for Pete's sake, buy it!" the exasperated husband said.

June, of course, knew her husband's strike zone. He disliked confrontation with his wife, however minor. All the lady had to do was concentrate on her goal.

You too can multiply your PCP on great projects or not-so-great projects, when you single-mindedly aim at the strike zone as June Perry did.

HOW THE BIG WHEELS WORK THE STRIKE ZONE

If anybody knows the miraculous secret of aiming for the strike zone, the big wheels do. They have a keen appreciation of PCP and they use it. These men and women are leaders: everybody recognizes them in every town, everywhere. They use these power techniques unfailingly, as they aim for the opponent's strike zone.

- They agree that the intensity and direction of personal command power is more important than having more of it than anybody else in the whole world.
- They act promptly to correct a mistake.
- They keep the door open.
- They play hard to get.
- They choose their targets for a purpose.

One more observation about the big wheels must be made before we go on. The big wheels are the thinkers and doers in society; they are the executives, the professionals, the leaders in every walk of life who make money, and get what they want through their own efforts. They strike when the iron is hot.

The big wheels pour on intense concentration and give explicit direction to their PCP to reach a goal. They rarely worry about how much power they may or may not have since a major part of their success is their willingness to give undivided attention to their projects as they make the most of their command power. Most people possess more power than they are willing to use. Yet the big wheels don't make this mistake; they use all the power at their disposal to get what they want, when they want it, right where they are, regardless of the situation or circumstances.

Furthermore, the big wheels don't waste time and power worrying about what might have been. When they make an error, they calmly and honestly appraise what went wrong, then redirect their PCP toward regaining the lost ground. This done, they launch a new power offensive. "Attack" is a term that the big wheels understand. However, they often pull it off in a most unobtrusive manner, with an adroit use of PCP since they are after more important things than scalps.

The big wheels like it at the top, so they direct all their energies and talents at getting there and staying there. But they do keep the door open, in case they have to fall back and regroup. They do not abandon common sense in a pique, needlessly antagonize associates, or leave a wake of disgruntled dupes snapping at their heels. They understand the wisdom of having a base to fall back on in case of a temporary miscalculation. It has happened, even to presidents.

The big wheels are adept at playing games when someone is bargaining for their power and services. When giant corporations, great institutions, and smart executives look for help, they look for strong individuals with demonstrable power and ability. The men they bargain with play hard to get. PCP is a commodity that is not easily found or cheaply bought: there is little excuse for you to ever sell yours cheaply.

Before the big wheels turn their PCP loose, they choose their specific targets. This is a most important characteristic of the big wheels. Did you know that the majority of the people in this land waste their power because they never really select a strike zone or decide what they want? Not the big wheels. They choose their target and aim at the strike zone with a particular goal in mind.

We have looked at five of the more obvious techniques and characteristics the big wheels use in the strike zone. See how many of these you can recognize in this story of two of the nation's biggest wheels who we will call Jones and Smith.

Jones was a wealthy man with ample command power. Nevertheless, he did have a problem involving millions of dollars and thousands of employees. He was the president and chief operating officer of one of the biggest corporations in an industry of vital importance to us all. But the family business he had inherited was in poor shape and losing ground. Although the problem was not of his own doing, it still made things no easier. But Jones was intelligent: he knew that he had to have additional power to solve his dilemma and this extra outside power could be found only in the form of another man with superior power. Jones, who knew the advantages of the secret strategy of aiming for the strike zone, set his sights on the best man in the industry: Mr. Smith.

Smith headed a giant company even larger than the mammoth one Jones presided over. When Mr. Jones approached Mr. Smith, he played hard to get. "Not interested," he said. But here power was dealing with power: Jones backed up and regrouped, and finally elicited a promise from Smith to at least look and see what he thought he could do with Jones' company. The end result was that Smith agreed to accept the challenge, but only on his terms which included stock options, fringe benefits galore, and a salary that was almost obscene. Smith also knew how to work the strike zone, and was well aware of how badly Jones needed him.

Since power can flow in more than one direction, both men got what they wanted. Smith gained more power, prestige, and money when he moved into his new job. In addition, Jones sacrificed no power. As a matter of fact, with this bold use of his command power, he landed his man, restored his mighty corporation to its place of leadership, and gained even more power for himself. There is a lesson here for all of us.

SELECTING THE RIGHT STRIKE ZONE

Selecting the strike zone is a first consideration. In deciding just where to direct your PCP, there are three primary items to take into account. They are:

- Identifying your adversary's weak spot.
- Directing your PCP at that spot.
- Timing.

Once you find an opponent's weak spot, you can have things your own way if you are not squeamish or hesitant. Select the time that is to *your* advantage. This usually means acting promptly since the sooner you identify and aim for the strike zone, the sooner you can expect results.

For example, there is a large, thriving church in our state, which once found itself with a controversial pastor. Some of the dissatisfied members found his weak spot: the man was inordinately fond of women other than his own wife. Consequently, it wasn't long until he was trapped in a compromising position with a member's wife, and the dissidents sent a committee to see him. Their ultimatum was "get out or we will expose you before the congregation and your family." With this kind of power aimed smack at his weak spot, he quickly caved in and left, to minister to a smaller church at a lesser salary. Cruel? It depends upon your viewpoint. Effective power strategy? Ask the preacher.

INSTANT POWER POINTERS

- Your opponent's weak spot is the strike zone.
- Be relentless as you identify the foe's strike zone.
- Do not broadcast ahead of time what you plan to do.
- The shot-gun approach wastes power.
- Aim directly and exclusively at the strike zone.
- Don't take off your shoes when you have to step on toes.
- Concentrate on your goal *only*.
- You can't hit the strike zone with confetti.
- Power can flow in more than one direction.
- Three steps essential in working the strike zone are:
    - (1) Identifying your adversary's weak spot.
    - (2) Aiming your PCP at that spot.
    - (3) Selecting the time that is to your advantage.

4

Using People: A Sure-Fire Way to Multiply Your Personal Command Power

There is no point in being euphemistic about the term "using people." A weaker expression would not bring the point home. Using people does not mean *misusing* people: it does mean that when you motivate, inspire, or even force people to do what you want, you can multiply your personal command power. Essentially, either you manipulate people with your own brand of power, or you will be manipulated by their power. If this thought disturbs you a bit, just remember that life is not a game. By and large, people are out to get what they want. And using people is a sure-fire way to multiply your power as you go after what you want.

Who needs people? You, and every ambitious man or woman, because people are channels of power and the instruments through which you can reach out and extend your own PCP. If you limit yourself to what you alone can do, you are building a wall around your power. If possible, use people with sweet consideration to get their cooperation. If not, put on the pressure as necessary. Otherwise, you will find yourself marching to somebody else's drum.

YOU CAN CHOOSE PEOPLE WHO CAN
MULTIPLY YOUR POWER

Not everyone you bump into has the qualifications to help multiply your PCP. For instance, although this hard fact many find difficult to accept, the most agreeable people are not always the ones who can be useful to you. To put it another way, the people you like most are not always the ones who can make the biggest contribution to your power. As you widen the base for your PCP, you will often find it necessary to reach over and beyond the meek obliging people with whom you would prefer to deal. The way to multiply your power is to concentrate on the particular individuals who can help you the most despite any personality defects they may suffer. You don't have to like or admire them; just choose the ones who can help you get the job done.

First, make yourself a qualifications checklist along these lines:

Name: Joe Muscle
Personal data: Manager Big Motor Freight Lines
Personality Traits: Big. Eager to please. Ambitious. Brags a
   bit. Somewhat defensive. Not always sure of himself.

What can this person do for me?

(a) Can expedite freight shipments.
(b) Can be used to effect better pick-up and delivery at
   the company dock.

Techniques to use on this person:

(a) Discuss possibility of doing more business with
   him if he comes through.
(b) Threaten to take company business elsewhere if he
   doesn't cooperate.
(c) Carry out threats if necessary.
(d) Use another freight company as a back-up choice,
   and make Joe aware that this option is open.

I'm a firm believer in the use of pen and paper when mapping people-strategy and making plans because when you put it on paper, you eliminate a lot of fuzziness and bring the concrete facts out before your eyes. However you do it, you should employ a method that guarantees your knowing enough about the person you plan to use to get him to do what you want. Pinpoint his weak spots, note his likes and dislikes, fears, and hang-ups. Then, take the psychological advantage this information affords you in the manipulation of your helper. Keep this thought on the front burner: the total idea is to multiply your PCP through the judicious use of people.

AVOIDING WASTING TIME ON THE WRONG PEOPLE

Here's another salient point: never spend your time and power on someone who can't help you get what you want. If you choose such subjects as these to motivate and manipulate, all you will reap will be frustration.

Tom Jeffries, a new salesman with a large costume jewelry outfit, had been instructed to go after the account of a thriving discount chain. Tom worked for three months on Gail Thompson, the lady whom the receptionist let him in to see on his first trip. Miss Thompson had been polite, encouraging, and pleasant, had listened to Tom, and had carefully looked over his samples, but she never bought. Finally, Tom went in to his manager to explain his lack of success—a most humiliating experience for any serious salesman.

Jack Winthrow, Tom's sales manager, arranged to call on the chain's headquarters with Tom. As soon as they arrived, they were ushered into Miss Thompson's office where she bubbled with sweetness and self-importance. But when Jack Winthrow saw that Gail Thompson was willing to talk about anything under the sun except a commitment to buy, he turned on a bit of PCP. "Miss Thompson, who is the person we must see to get a buying decision today?" he asked. "Oh," said Miss Thompson, sweet as ever, "that would be Pamela Howell. I'm her assistant. Let me ring her for you." One hour later, the two men walked out with a substantial order.

As soon as they were out of earshot Tom said, "Boy, I sure goofed somewhere along the line, didn't I? You made that look so easy."

"Tom," answered his sales manager, "you made only one mistake with this account, but it was a serious one."

"Tell me!" implored Tom.

"You wasted your time and the company's money by trying to work the wrong party. There was no way that Gail Thompson could have given you an order. I hope that you have already made a mental note not to waste time again with anyone who can't help you get what you want."

Tom, of course, learned his lesson. As a strong and experienced salesman, he now makes certain that he works only with people he can use profitably.

You are the only one fully acquainted with your situation, your circumstances, your goal, and the circle of people you can reach. This vital information is your strategic edge in choosing the right people to use.

HOW DR. S. A. PRITCHFORD USED PEOPLE TO DOUBLE THE SIZE OF MEDICAL CENTER HOSPITAL

Dr. Sam Pritchford appreciates this secret of picking people you can use from those right around you. He was able to double the size of Medical Center Hospital using this prize technique.

Dr. Pritchford had spent twenty years working with and helping to build Medical Center Hospital, and was a respected, prominent man with proven influence and power. However, his beloved hospital was now running out of room and was short of funds. As the city had grown, the patient load had shot upward. The manpower and facilities at the hospital were hard put to handle the load. Dr. Pritchford made up his mind to alleviate the situation: he would have to use other people.

As a medical man and a recognized administrator, Dr. Pritchford knew that people will treat you about as you expect to be treated, will cooperate with you to the extent that you expect them to cooperate, and will be used about as much as you expect them to be used. Armed with this secret arsenal of people-facts, Dr. Pritchford launched his campaign. He made a list of the most powerful, wealthy and influential people in town who he would use to multiply his PCP and double the size of Medical Center Hospital.

The first person he approached was a hard-nosed businessman named Lester Knox. His old friend greeted him with, "Well what do you want this time, Sam?"

"One hundred thousand dollars from you," replied the doctor.

"What do you think I am, Sam? The First National Bank?" This was more or less the reply Dr. Pritchford had anticipated.

"No, better than that," said Dr. Pritchford. "The $100,000 isn't all I expect from you. I want you to help me raise $5,000,000. Here's a list of people you can contact. I'll help, but I'm counting on you to put across this project to double the size of our hospital. Then I want one more thing from you."

"What's that?" Mr. Knox wanted to know.

"I want you to act as treasurer for our campaign," stated the doctor.

Mr. Knox protested weakly, but the strong-willed Dr. Pritchford hung on. When the interview ended, Dr. Sam had Mr. Knox's pledge for $100,000, his agreement to act as treasurer for the fund-raising drive, and Mr. Knox's secretary was already contacting prospective contributors and volunteers from Dr. Pritchford's list. The good doctor's command power was multiplying fast: within three months, the money was raised and construction underway. As you can see, Dr. Pritchford's secret prescription of using people to multiply PCP is strong medicine.

HOW TO IDENTIFY AND INFLUENCE KEY PEOPLE

The more people you can influence, the more you can multiply your PCP. Remember: when we say "more people," we do not mean any and all people you may happen to meet. Precisely, the more "key" people you can influence, the faster you can multiply your personal command power. When you influence/use the key person in any group, he or she will spread your influence and power to the others. By asking a few, simple, people-questions, you can identify these key people and avoid wasting time and power. Ask yourself:

- Is this person in a position to help me?
- Is this person influential in his own right?

- Does he command respect?
- Does he have power of his own that I can tap?
- Is he smart enough to get what I want done?
- Have I developed the proper strategy to control and use this person?

If your answer is yes to these and any other searching questions applicable to your particular case, then you have your sights on the right party. Go ahead and work on using them to your advantage.

DON'T VICTIMIZE YOURSELF

As you launch your power drive to influence and use people, don't expect instant applause. When you step on the obstinate toes in your path, you will be subject to

- Angry retorts
- Hurt looks
- Surprised reactions
- Nervous protests
- Pleas of innocence
- Offended scowls
- Little, bribing concessions
- Empty, half-hearted threats
- Uncomplimentary name-calling
- A few crocodile tears.

Don't be trapped into feeling guilty just because you have decided to use your personal power to get ahead and fulfill your goals. Don't dignify contrived little dramas by showing undue concern over them; to do so would undermine your influence and cripple your power.

Pam Hall decided to pick up her business career when her children got old enough not to need her full attention. But her husband protested that her place was in the home, and the children screamed that daddy was right. However, when Pam brought home her first $2000 commission check which she earned as a real estate salesperson, calm and peace soon settled upon the household. Her husband said it was reassuring to have a second income, and the children beamed with pride.

Pam still works outside the home, and the family has never been neglected. This persistent lady fulfilled her goal without causing any hardship. Instead, she substantially increased her personal contribution to her family's well-being. Could this have come about had Pam victimized herself when she ran into all that resistance and noise?

YOU HAVE TO DISH IT OUT

You have to dish it out in order to multiply your PCP by using other people. This is not to say that massacre is synonymous with power. Instead, it means that firm decisions and aggressive actions are indicated, and that you should not be deterred by a few cries of outrage when you set about to multiply your PCP. To keep this thought constantly in focus, let's look at two relative points.

1. Don't be overwhelmed that people may be evaluating you.

Of course you are going to be evaluated. You will be taken apart every day of your life, whether you use people or people are using you. Don't waver; remember that you have power you were born with. Using it aggressively is your concern.

Be glad that you are being evaluated, weighed, criticized, and analyzed. It is a good sign because only the weak and incompetent escape this exacting scrutiny. This burning examination puts your PCP in the spotlight and the extra recognition you can gain from this will actually help you move faster as you motivate, influence, and use people.

2. Don't worry about a power blackout.

Worry and nervous misgivings contribute nothing to PCP. If you quiver and quaver as you face a person or circumstance requiring power, you will rob yourself. Even the most powerful and experienced of us sometimes feel the strain on our personalities as we act to influence people to do our bidding. No matter how strong and how powerful you may become, you will still be subject to a few mortal afflictions. Accept that much as a fact of life; just don't let it interfere with your campaign to multiply your PCP. That attitude precludes any worry about a power blackout.

MAKING DOMINATION THE KEY
TO CONSTRUCTIVE USE OF PEOPLE

One definition of domination is "to exert the supreme determining or guiding influence on," and another is "control." Obviously, absolute control is the order of the day when you plan to multiply your personal command power. The way to control a person or a situation is to doggedly refuse to be swayed from your course. When you hang in and use strategy to keep people on track despite provocation, grumbling, or other distractions, then you are in charge, as the following example shows.

Warren Palen, a compelling and effective speaker accustomed to close attention and cooperation, was conducting a seminar for sales and management personnel at the home office of his firm's largest account. But in this isolated case, Ben Parnum, a veteran salesman in the group, insisted on distracting the man on his left and the man on his right with irritating stage whispers. He annoyed the audience in general and Warren Palen in particular, but Warren maintained control by a fine display of command power. He simply stopped his presentation and waited for the culprit to look up. Then he said, "Mr. Parnum, let me explain something to you. If you are going to be rude enough to disrupt this meeting, I am going to call everybody's attention to the problem each time you do so. For both our sakes, I hope you can remember that."

Warren Palen then proceeded as if nothing had happened, and the rest of the meeting went smoothly.

It is worth noting the ripple effect this exercise in domination produced. As soon as the meeting ended, Ben Parnum apologized and Parnum's superiors expressed their appreciation to Mr. Palen for the way he had handled Parnum. Several of Ben's co-workers congratulated Warren and confided that Ben had no doubt profited immensely from the experience.

Consider this: had Ben Parnum been allowed to persist in his rude behavior, would he have learned anything? Would the other participants have been able to work with Warren Palen? Would Warren have fulfilled his obligation to his audience, his company, or himself? Finally, what would have happened to Warren Palen's command power had he allowed himself to be knocked off course?

DOMINATION IS FOR EVERY DAY

Domination is the secret key to multiplying your PCP in your daily affairs as well as in the unexpected events that will hit you like a wall of water. When viewed together, what goes on in your life on a daily basis is the bigger part of the whole fabric. Don't save domination for only the monumental moments in your life; it is a waste to put it in mothballs until you have a crisis on your hands.

Wade Ousley always spent his Saturdays mowing his yard and keeping the homestead in good shape. True, he had an able bodied sixteen-year-old son, Leslie, but he was always "too busy." Wade realized he was doing the boy no favors by excusing him, so he used a touch of domination and set the matter straight. He told Leslie that until he started mowing the yard and assuming some responsibility, there would be no more allowance and no more car privileges. Since then, Wade has had almost every Saturday free to pursue his other interests, and his wife enjoys the extra time with her husband. Using his own son in a responsible manner has strengthened family ties and made for harmony all around. It's no big thing, but a classic example of how domination can be put to work to whip irritating little problems as well as major threats.

HOW THE CONSTRUCTIVE USE OF PEOPLE
MULTIPLIES YOUR PCP

The central word and idea in your strategy to use people is *constructive.* This healthy motive is in direct opposition to the destructive use of people. The former multiplies your power and spreads your PCP to broaden your power base, while the latter may serve as a temporary end, which in the long run becomes a negative force. Destructive people-use will shrivel your power to short-term, and often petty projects. Nonetheless, operating in a constructive manner is using people for stronger motives than merely putting them down. You can use people to get what you want without coming away with bloodied hands, a violated conscience, or a soiled reputation. And you can do it with fire and electricity.

The constructive use of people always multiplies your PCP because it:

- Spreads your influence.
- Extends your power beyond your immediate presence.
- Enhances your reputation as a go-getter.
- Paves the way for new opportunities.
- Attracts strong friends.
- Gives you an army of support.
- Makes it easier to get what you want.

Use people to multiply your personal command power. You owe this much to yourself and to the people around you.

INSTANT POWER POINTERS

- Don't be squeamish about the term "using people."
- You need people.
- Choose people who can multiply your personal command power.

- The most agreeable people are not always the most useful to you.
- Don't waste time on someone who can't help you.
- The more key people you use, the more you will multiply your PCP.
- Do not victimize yourself.
- You will be evaluated.
- Domination is the key.

5

Power Secrets That Get People to Do What You Want

The best method you can use to multiply your personal command power is to *use* it to get other people to do what you want. Euphemistic terms frequently describe people who are able to manipulate and move others in whatever direction they desire; among these adjectives are such words as charisma, likeability, smoothness, charm, and similar glossy words and expressions that express the speaker's awe and admiration for someone with a strong personality. The most appropriate term, however, is personal command power since it is the real force that gets people to do what you want, regardless of their personal characteristics or quirks.

USE DIFFERENT POWER TACTICS
FOR DIFFERENT PEOPLE

All people are different: we are cast from different molds, and march to different drummers. A power secret that gets one person or group to do what you want, may have to be modified to get the next person or the next audience to do your bidding.

Therefore, exercising people-judgment is an important part of PCP: it is a real power strategy.

Here are some of the personality types you may encounter, together with applicable power secrets that you can use to bring them into line:

● Indifferent personalities

These can often be the most difficult cases because they have no firm convictions of their own, and simply do not seem to care one way or the other.

To deal with the indifferent personality, you must provide motivation by showing them how and why they will benefit from following you. Often it will be more important to make this vacillating type feel that he will be highly uncomfortable if he does not comply to your wishes. You can effectively deal with this insulated character by breaking down your campaign into two segments:

(a) Here is what will happen if you do as I am suggesting.

(b) Here is what will happen if you fail to act in the positive way I outline for you.

A highly successful accounting firm gets indifferent prospective customers to follow their guidance by using this secret technique. In essence they say, "Okay, if you do as we have outlined, you will have control of your business. Our computer readouts will show you exactly where you stand each month, and will show you what needs to be done to keep your business sound and growing. Or, on the other hand, you can continue to worry about an unbalanced inventory, overpayment of tax, unproductive employees, and questionable profit margins."

You can vary this two-part power technique to fit the situation as you meet indifferent people. It will move them off dead center, and get them to do what you know they should do.

● Abrasive personalities

The abrasive personality will want to give you a hard time, even if it is obvious that his salvation lies in doing exactly what you want. His language and behavior is coarse and abusive, but this is usually nothing more than a screen behind which an insecure person hides. The quickest and best way to handle this character is to establish your position in the only way this type understands—simply refine his coarse technique and meet fire with fire. However, you don't have to use foul language or gutter tactics to make your point.

When an employee, a construction foreman, tried to intimidate Keith Dodson with abusive language and an abrasive outburst, Keith got up and faced him, saying, "Cowboy, I don't know what you are trying to prove, but you are not scaring anybody. I hope for both our sakes that you won't be foolish enough to permit another such outburst."

The man apologized and Keith graciously let him off the hook in front of his co-workers. As a result of his firm stand, Mr. Dodson has had little trouble getting the whole-hearted cooperation of his crew. They now actually seem to enjoy doing what he wants them to do because his no-nonsense power play earned their full respect. This all resulted when Keith Dodson refined a coarse man's technique, stopped him with his own medicine, and made him do as he asked.

• Incompetent individuals

There is small point in working at getting the incompetent to do what you want. What will you gain by having a bunch of incompetents working in your behalf? It is far better to use your command power to line up capable associates who can further your interests as well as their own.

• Docile personalities

Using your PCP on the docile type has its problems because he is usually too easily manipulated, and while you can quickly influence him with your stronger personality, so can just about everybody else. This fragments him and sends him off into all directions like a leaf in the wind which, of course, destroys his usefulness to you. Not only that, but this characteristic renders him a highly ineffective individual in whatever he does. So do not waste a lot of your time and power here. If you have a minor job to be done, this type might qualify, but for more worthwhile projects, go after stronger individuals with whom your PCP really pays off.

● Strong personalities

When you manipulate, lead, drive, and influence the strong types, you have added firepower to your PCP. Strong people have power of their own: they get things done. When you use your command power to control and direct strong people, you can attain your goals more readily and expand your influence accordingly.

Strong characters are more easily led than driven. To get them working in your behalf, simply lay an opportunity in their path. It is a mistake to offer a strong man or woman a bribe to motivate them to do as you want. Instead, you must stick a pin in their self-interest. Remember, the best approach is the direct approach, so you can say, in effect, "Here is an opportunity for you to make a lot of money or win this contest, or be the leader in this campaign, or become the envy of all your co-workers. It takes work and special ability. If you think you can handle it, here is what must be done."

When you use this power-play approach, you will have:

(a) Opened a challenge in which a strong individual can excel.
(b) Emphasized that hard work is required.
(c) Complimented your prospective helper by stressing the need for special ability.
(d) Put the responsibility on him by indirectly asking if he can handle the job.
(e) Have let him know that you are the boss right from the start.

This is an effective power technique that you can use in many situations when dealing with strong characters.

● Hostile personalities

The hostile type is more suspicious than antagonistic. He is showing outrage as a defensive gesture. This type has probably had his feet kicked out from under him a few times in the past and now feels compelled to put up an angry, distrustful front to protect himself. Though he will never admit it, especially to himself, he really is afraid.

If you have need for the hostile type, and if he can be of service to you, don't be scared off too easily. The fact that he has enough spunk to show some fire indicates that he might be aggressive enough to accomplish something for you. But you can't pussyfoot with this type. The best way to handle him and get him doing what you want is to blast off with a show of power. Use the same basic technique here as with the strong character: let him know from the start who is going to be the boss. At the same time, dangle the rewards before him, just as when manipulating a strong individual. Keep in mind that the hostile type isn't mad at *you*, he's upset with the whole world. What he really needs is a strong leader to bring some sense and order into his life. Do this, and you will have a loyal, lasting follower.

Every individual offers a singular challenge to the power-minded. Vary your approach and method to suit the particular case, as shown in dealing with the types already outlined. You will then be channelling your PCP where it will move people to do what you want them to do, when you want them to do it.

HOW TO KEEP YOUR PEOPLE POWER HOT

The more experienced you become at forcefully applying your PCP, the more you will appreciate its truly constructive force. Like all power tools, it demands careful handling. The following are some power secrets designed to keep your power hot while you work on getting people to do what you want.

• Don't be too obvious

You can imagine what would happen if you walked up to a healthy man or woman and said, "Hey, I'm gonna make you do what I want!"

Fireworks would erupt like the Fourth of July, and your PCP would fizzle like a dying ember. But you can use power and make strong, compelling statements without starting a fight or having any fireworks. With a proper mixture of force and the promise of reward, together with a picture of the consequences of ignoring your directions, you can win your way and have fun doing it. Here are the keys:

(1) Act with authority.
(2) Be fair but exacting.
(3) Take charge from the start.
(4) Spell it all out.

People respect authority. This is easy to understand because of the very definition of authority: an individual who is an expert and has the power to influence or command thought, opinion, or behavior in other people. It follows, then, that as a person imbued with PCP, you will be expected to act with authority when you work on getting people to do what you want. Nothing less will suffice.

It's important to be fair, but the effect will be lost unless you are also explicit about whatever it is you want your helpers to do. No one can work effectively for you until he understands exactly what you want from him.

In your campaign to get people to do what you want, it is vital that you take charge from the start. There is no other way to be fully successful in motivating others to do your bidding.

As previously indicated, you must spell everything out. The people working in your behalf will lose interest and drift away if your point is not clearly and forcefully made, so make notes for yourself ahead of time. Your objectives must first be organized in your own mind, then you can give your instructions precisely as you motivate those around you. Remember that if there is any way for you to be misunderstood, you will be.

Frank Bilyeau is a plant manager. He has no formal engineering degree, but he knows how to get people to follow his instructions. For example, Frank had a worker who was occasionally prone to absenteeism. Frank put a stop to the problem by saying, "Jim, if you want to work here you will have to be here every day and on time. You understand, don't you?"

Frank acted with authority, was fair, but direct, took full charge, and spelled everything out. Note: Jim hasn't been absent or tardy since.

In another instance, Frank removed two unproductive workers from a production line by getting the supervisor to do exactly what he wanted. "Orville," Frank said, "our studies have shown that you need only ten people instead of twelve on this line. Figure out how you want to realign your schedule, then tell me in the morning which two workers you want me to reassign."

Same technique, same positive statements, same positive results. As illustrated, you don't have to make an issue of the fact that you are going to get people to comply. Use the secret power keys we've discussed, along with your built-in power skills, the same way Frank Bilyeau does. This will keep your power burning without unnecessary hassle.

● Use power without being overbearing.

Some people will respond only when pressured. Pressure will keep your power hot, but only if you don't let it seem to or actually become overbearing. You can exert power by being persistent, aggressive, insistent, and demanding when necessary. The trick is to accomplish your goals without arousing undue antagonism. To use pressure and get people to do what you want without being overbearing, try the following ideas:

● Speak the language of the other person.

Unless the people whose cooperation you seek can understand you, they cannot do what you want. If you use fancy language or speak patronizingly to your prospective helpers, they will consider you snobbish and overbearing. If your speech is stilted and affected, they won't take you seriously. Use easily understood words, short, concise sentences, and powerful statements such as:

"Here is how to do it."

"This is the best way for you and for me."

"Here's how to do the job quickly."

"This will make you the most money."

"This will get you a promotion fast."

"You lose if you don't act now."

● **Let the other person feel comfortable.**

This is important when you're using subtle pressure to bring him around because he will then work harder for you. You can succeed in this by showing him what he will gain by cooperating with you. While you are pushing him in your direction, minimize the risks he might encounter; make him comfortable by dwelling on the positive aspects of doing your bidding. Operating on this positive plane will keep your helpers hot.

POWER SECRETS THAT KEEP PCP
A CONSTRUCTIVE FORCE

Being positive and constructive does not mean that you should ever use milk-sop tactics to get people to do what you want. The positive, constructive method is the preferred way; it is not the only way. On occasion, you will have to step on toes to get what you want. Be sweet and constructive *only* if circumstances permit.

Fortunately, forceful tact will usually accomplish your goals. Two further points worth remembering as you do your best to motivate and manipulate people follow.

● **Show a bit of sympathy for the other person's viewpoint.**

This is a good technique, but be sure to keep your viewpoint out front. For example, when the other person expresses his viewpoint, you can nod sympathetically and say, "Interesting. . . ." Then go right ahead and drive home why your idea is better for both of you.

● **Get right into your project.**

Dilly-dallying is no way to get anybody to do anything for you. Get right into your project when you want to motivate and maneuver someone into your corner. For instance, say: "I expect your help now." Don't say: "If you can possibly help, I would like to get started today." Say: "This project requires an immediate decision. Let's get moving." Don't say: "There's sort of a hurry. I hope that you can make up your mind soon."

THE ODDS ARE IN YOUR FAVOR

This is the case when you set about getting people to do what you want. People respect power; they respect the man who knows how to use it and who has the will to do so. The following analytical chart based on my observation and experience shows how the odds are stacked.

3% will recognize what you are doing.

10% will wonder why you work so hard.

5% will be excited by your drive and determination.

10% will try to follow your example.

2% will consider you a threat.

70% will admire and respect you.

Take a second look at those statistics. They give you every reason to be optimistic as you work on getting people to do what you want. A second look reveals the following:

- The 3% who recognize what you are doing won't be unduly alarmed. They will fall in line as soon as you convince them that what you want is to their advantage.
- The 10% are merely lazy. They will require a little more prodding before they move in your direction.
- The 5% you excite with your power will be putty in your hands.
- The 10% who try to follow your example will be eager to work with you.
- The 2% who will consider you a threat will nonetheless envy you for your PCP. This gives you a chance to use your power on these people.

- The 70% who admire and respect you will readily cooperate with you. All they need is assurance that you are working for the mutual good of all parties. By now, you have already been exposed to enough technique and procedure to handle this detail.

Use the power secrets that we have discussed, along with some that will be uniquely your own. You will be surprised at how willingly people will respond by doing what you ask. The odds are stacked in your favor.

INSTANT POWER POINTERS

- Getting people to do what you want is the quickest way to multiply your PCP.
- Different people require different power tactics.
- People-judgment is a power secret.
- Put the emphasis on getting strong, competent people to do what you want.
- Every individual offers a rewarding challenge.
- Don't be obvious.
- Use pressure diplomatically.
- Speak the language of the other person.
- Show the other person what is in it for him.
- Avoid milk-sop tactics.
- Forceful tact will win.
- Do not delay—get right into your project.
- The odds are in your favor.

6

How Enthusiasm Explodes Your
Personal Command Power

More has probably been written and said about the importance of enthusiasm than about any other personality trait. There is a reason. Enthusiasm has magic-like results, time after time. Salesmen rely upon it, managers and executives extol its virtues, and leaders use it daily to motivate, control, and guide masses of people. Enthusiasm's power will help heat up and energize your personal command power.

HOW ENTHUSIASM HEATS UP PCP

PCP cannot amount to much unless people respond to it; in order to do so, those around you must believe in it, recognize it, and be strongly impressed with it. Enthusiasm enables you to create this needed atmosphere. For example, have you ever seen anyone who was a power to be reckoned with have a gloomy expression or show self-doubts? On the other hand, we have all seen men and women gather around an aggressive, enthusiastic person like flies around a honey pot.

If you enthusiastically radiate power, the people around

71

you can't help but feel it and respond to it because enthusiasm inspires confidence.

However, not everybody is born with a bubbling out-going personality, but anybody who works at it can feel and be enthusiastic. To acquire this enthusiasm that adds fire to your personal command power, try the following suggestions.

First, when you act enthusiastically, you will become eager because your heart beats faster, your eyes are brighter, and you look better. Your actions stir up the juices that make you enthusiastic, so you don't have to fake it. It's there in your make-up, just as all the other ingredients of power are inside you.

It will also help if you know what you are excited about. Enthusiasm is more than a balloon of hot air, a toothy smile, and a bubbling torrent of words. You must know your product, whether it be an idea, a political candidate, a candy bar, or a steam ship. The more you know about something, the more reasons you have for effervescing about it. Study your product or project and become the authority on it. Then it will be easy for you to act enthusiastically about it.

Fred Rainwater sold candy for years. He was competent and liked his job, but he didn't become marketing director for his company until he studied the history and romance of candy-making. The more he learned, the more enthusiastically he acted. His sales shot upward and his superiors took notice of this genuinely charismatic leader. Fred acknowledges that he didn't get promoted because he worked harder; he always had. Instead, it was due to his enthusiasm for his product as he learned more and more about it. It will work the same way for you.

The second point to be made is this: if you want to explode your PCP with enthusiasm, don't wait for a flash of inspiration before you begin acting enthusiastically. Not many songs would have been written if the musician always waited for inspiration before going to work. Professional writers, artists, business leaders, and other power-minded personalities all concede that they must seem excited even if they aren't at the moment. The key word is *act*. Once you act, enthusiasm will follow as naturally as day follows night.

Acting enthusiastically will heat up your PCP, and those you seek to motivate will feel the heat too.

HOW TO ATTRACT ENTHUSIASTIC FOLLOWERS

There is a sure way to motivate others: look and sound enthusiastic yourself. By doing so, you will inspire those around you to identify with you. This ability to inspire is one of the prize secrets of PCP. Your own enthusiasm will be catching, and inspire others to follow you.

For example, the Women's Council of a local real estate association was losing members and barely functioning until Jane Privett, an eager young realty associate, was named president. She presided with optimism and excitement and soon old members began attending the meetings once more, new members joined the association, and the programs were lively again. The membership assumed their responsibilities, and within one year, this association achieved national recognition and acclaim. Jane Privett's enthusiasm had drawn helpers to her. This naturally exploded her PCP into the national spotlight.

Alfred Carbow had been handed the difficult assignment of rebuilding a huge department store's appliance department which, under the old manager, had slipped into a low-profit, low-volume syndrome. Alfred came in as if he had been promoted to the hottest division in the store. He exuded enthusiasm and demonstrated personally to the six sales people under his supervision how enthusiasm moved people, by having them watch quietly while he sold the highest priced units in the department. Carbow's people followed his example and within six months, the department's volume tripled with the high-end goods accounting for 80% of the department's volume. His ebullience transformed a mediocre sales force into a group of productive followers. To this day, Alfred Carbow still relies on this method to explode his PCP while leading his followers into ever-growing production.

HOW INTROVERT HENRY TODD EXPLODED HIS PCP WITH ENTHUSIASM

Self-discipline is the first step in developing enthusiasm and power. This is a secret that you should chip in stone, as

Henry Todd will attest. Henry was young, intelligent, reasonably good looking, and a diligent worker. Yet he was so shy, he couldn't tell a stranger his name without blushing. But, Henry did possess some inner resources. His common sense told him that if he were ever to get anywhere socially or professionally, he would have to overcome his painful shyness. He decided that the best way to do this was to force himself to talk before groups of people. This in itself was evidence of the latent PCP Henry had been smothering with his shyness.

Once Henry had made his decision, he went to his church's Sunday School superintendent and explained that he wanted to teach a class, which was welcome news. Henry was immediately given a class of young married couples his own age. He studied all week, prepared for his first teaching assignment, then suffered the agonies of the damned as he stood before the class and taught. Somehow he survived and had not suffered the fatal stroke he fully expected.

The next Sunday it was easier; after that it was a joy. Henry began looking forward to each session with the class and was elated when it began to grow. His enthusiasm knew no bounds.

It was inevitable that Henry should begin to exercise his new-found PCP in other ways. Aggressively, he sought new friends, eagerly accepted more challenging responsibilities, and became known as a powerful inspirational speaker. Then he decided to become a preacher. Henry had exploded his PCP with enthusiasm: the rewards were beyond anything he had dared dream. Today he is widely sought after in his chosen profession. If you are fortunate, you may have a chance to see this dynamic man who exploded his PCP by using his keenly disciplined enthusiasm.

YOUR ENTHUSIASM MAKES YOUR COMMAND POWER BELIEVABLE

When your PCP is operating successfully, people will believe you. Your enthusiasm shows that you have faith in what you are saying, in what you are doing, and it underscores your self-confidence. Your own attitude is a testimonial which instills confidence and support in those you want to influence. People can't help but think that if you are *that* enthusiastic and are willing to work *that* hard at it, then there must be something to it.

This is sound reasoning.

ENTHUSIASM IS CONTAGIOUS

A good reason to align yourself with enthusiastic associates is that zeal is contagious. It rubs off on you, molds your behavior, your ideas, and your character. Similarly, the PCP you use on people is also contagious. This combination of enthusiasm and power spreads your influence, enhances your reputation, helps you get what you want, and adds zest and excitement to whatever you do. Your eagerness makes you fun to be with, so your associates feel privileged to join in on your enthusiasm. Your PCP, fired by zeal, paves the way for you to guide, lead, direct, and use people.

INTERACTION ADDS POWER

We have stressed the point that people are necessary for power. What does it matter to anyone how much power a hermit might have with nobody around to use it on? This is also true of enthusiasm. How can enthusiasm explode your PCP if you show it only when you are alone? Therefore, you must interact with people in order to explode your power.

John Ridolfe explained recently, in a speech before town officials and Chamber of Commerce leaders, why he considered it imperative for power-driven individuals to interact intensely with other people. His point was that if you are the only one with any enthusiasm or power in an enterprise or among an assembly of people, your problem is compounded. He feels that you must operate through other intelligent, aggressive, enthusiastic, power-conscious people. This is how your own PCP will be strengthened; because enthusiasm and power is contagious. It explodes personal command power.

Hang on to this power secret. It has made John Ridolfe a powerful man and it will do no less for you.

ENTHUSIASM IS YOUR PERSONAL POWER ELEMENT

Enthusiasm cannot be considered impersonal: it is a basic part of your power make-up. It is part of your living, working personality, and its strength and use depends on you since it is yours alone. It can explode your personal command power the day you ignite it.

HOW TO FIND ENTHUSIASM EVERY DAY

It is sheer fantasy to think that you might awaken each morning feeling so zealous that you can hardly stand it. But you can begin each day excitedly by following our earlier technique and *acting* enthusiastically every morning. When you discipline yourself to do this, you will feel power beginning to surge through you *before* you get to the breakfast table. Personality experts will tell you that the way you act will basically affect the way you feel. This is a positive, constructive fact, and something you can use to avoid depriving yourself for even a day.

HOW SANDY REED WON A PROMOTION
PLUS TWO MARRIAGE PROPOSALS

Miss Reed was one among many girls who worked in the office of a big insurance company. Although she was one face among many, there was this difference: Sandy was ambitious.

Sandy's dormant command power began to stir. She decided to put herself ahead of the pack by becoming the best qualified and most enthusiastic worker in the office.

As she charted her campaign, Sandy observed that a number of the girls dressed inappropriately, tottered about on high heels, and grumbled over petty matters. Some of them watched the clock and took off like a jet at the end of each day.

Sandy gave her PCP her own special treatment. She sought responsibility, asked no favors, and enthusiastically devoted herself to the job at hand. Her disciplined, assertive conduct attracted attention both in and out of the office. Soon she became a desirable social partner as well as a valued employee. At the next evaluation period, Sandy was promoted to supervisor. Then, Dick Hamilton and Elmo Hardgrove suddenly discovered that she was the only girl in the world and both proposed. Sandy, however, graciously declined. She was enjoying her new-found personal power too much to abandon her career.

Exploding your PCP with enthusiasm can have most gratifying results, as Sandy will tell you.

10 REASONS WHY ENTHUSIASM EXPLODES PCP

There are many reasons why enthusiasm will explode your PCP. Study the following ten and put them to work for *you* today.

(1) Enthusiasm creates excitement and action.

It is impossible for you to sit still when you are bubbling with enthusiasm: you just can't wait for something to happen and then react to it. When you are boiling, you make things happen and you make them happen your way. Enthusiasm creates excitement in yourself and in those near you. And you can draw people into the action and under the direction of your power. The urge to move, accomplish, and win is overwhelming, as the record books all show. Take advantage of this personal power source and set some records of your own.

(2) Enthusiasm inspires confidence.

Enthusiasm builds self-confidence, but the real beauty of this power secret is that enthusiasm inspires other people to have the utmost faith in you and your ability. When you act enthusiastically, it is obvious to the associates you seek to motivate and control that power is flowing all through you. They sense it and see it because your inspired self-confidence is sending out the message. Thus, your enthusiasm gives you a power hot-line right to your goals.

(3) Enthusiasm labels you a leader.

Enthusiasm labels you a leader as if it were a red tag around your neck. Losers are not enthusiastic; winners are, but winners work at it, practice it and plan it. They study, establish goals, map strategy, and select the right people to influence and use.

One young salesman felt that his lack of enthusiasm was due to his poor sales and complained that only the leaders seemed to have reason to be excited. But then a wiser man told him that he had the shoe on the wrong foot; the truth of the matter was that his lack of sales was due to his blasé attitude. Leaders were enthusiastic before they reached the top, and further, enthusiasm was what put the leaders into the top ranks in the first place! He shared his knowledge of the secret power of enthusiasm with his dejected young friend and showed him many of the techniques found in this book. Today, that young salesman is an enthusiastic leader himself.

(4) Enthusiasm makes people want to identify with you.

This is because it creates an aura of success and power, which gives the people you seek to control a feeling of security. It also lifts their prestige and self-esteem, which is more than enough reason to dismiss any negative notions about using people. They want to identify with an enthusiastic power figure. You are that person.

(5) Enthusiasm eliminates fear and doubt.

Try this: the next time you have a problem, tackle it with a load of enthusiasm even if you must force yourself. As you work on the solution in this manner, you will find that fear and doubt will be replaced by confidence and power. Enthusiasm is a power element that has a proven history. It will put you in condition to handle any opposition or obstacle.

(6) Enthusiasm generates extra energy.

Depression and non-performance will rob your vitality and sap your power. On the other hand, when you take charge and inject enthusiasm into your personality, you will gain extra energy. Enthusiasm takes your mind off the negative and gets your power working on what you want from whomever you want it. Enthusiasm gives you and the people you lead 20-20 vision to see results. It is reason and power, sweetened with a positive attitude that creates an onrush of added energy. If you wonder about this, let me ask you something: how many enthusiastic people have you seen lately who were tired, weary, or discouraged?

(7) Enthusiasm gives you added stamina.

Enthusiasm gives added stamina to your PCP in the same way it generates extra energy. It gives you the power to hang in there until you get what you want. Remember, nobody ever quit when enthusiasm was high. Keep this in mind and you will never fall short.

(8) Enthusiasm eliminates boredom.

Boredom is a thief that stifles power. Enthusiasm routs the thief because it puts your mind on results rather than emphasizing procedure. There is no way to eliminate all routine work and every annoying detail as you turn your power loose on goal after goal, but you can take the boredom out of it by focusing on the whole ball of wax. Remember, you and you alone control your attitude. Load yours up with vitality and boredom will never rob you of your power.

(9) Enthusiasm makes work a pleasure.

Since power demands work, the ambitious power-seeker burns a lot of calories. The men or women exploding their PCP know what they want and where they are going, which in itself is enough to make work a pleasure. When your ever-growing PCP is loaded with enthusiasm, your work will never be drudgery.

(10) Enthusiasm keeps PCP at peak efficiency.

As you practice enthusiasm, you will make your own positive judgments about it and you will discover more reasons why it keeps your PCP at a high level. You will find new ways to maintain and harness your own personal enthusiasm. This is the secret lubricant that greases the wheels of power.

AN ENTHUSIASM POWER CHECK

To see how far you have progressed, answer each question mentally. As you mull each one over in your head, you will discover which areas you need to work on with enthusiasm, in order to make the most of your PCP.

(1) Are you eager to take action when you want something?

(2) Do you like to win?

(3) Are you a self-starter?

(4) Do you set your own goals?

(5) Do you make your own decisions?

(6) Do you base your power strategy on what you want?

(7) Do you dig right in again after a temporary set-back?

(8) Do you enjoy controlling people?

(9) Do you ignore big-mouthed critics?

(10) Do you seek the responsibilities of a compelling leader?

(11) Are you attracting strong helpers?

(12) Do the people you choose respond with enthusiasm?

If you can answer "yes" to ten of these questions, your enthusiasm is in good shape. If you can answer "yes" to all twelve, then enthusiasm is exploding your PCP like a rocket.

INSTANT POWER POINTERS

- Your emotional state rubs off on those with whom you deal.
- When you act enthusiastically, you will become enthusiastic.
- Don't wait for inspiration to be enthusiastic.
- Enthusiasm attracts strong followers.

- Self-discipline is the first step in developing enthusiasm and power.
- Enthusiasm is contagious.
- Enthusiasm is a personal power element.
- The way you act affects the way you feel.
- Enthusiasm keeps PCP at peak efficiency.
- Enthusiasm will explode your PCP like fireworks.

7

Power Secrets That Create a Strong First Impression

The first sixty seconds are the best and often the only time to make a power impression. Each time you meet a new person or face a new group, the first minute is crucial. In that time, you must establish your identity to create a strong first impression.

To fully appreciate the importance of a strong impression, think back to the people you have met. How many of them that came on like wooden horses do you still have as friends? How many of their names can you still recall? Do you remember anything about them except that they irritated or bored you?

One of the specifics of personal command power is the ability to make a strong first impression. This power secret makes everything else easier.

INSTANT DOMINANCE = POWER IMPRESSION

Dominance is most effective when put to work with the first handshake; the first eye-ball to eye-ball confrontation. Instant domination not only creates a power impression, it saves you the agony and embarrassment of having to go back and cover lost ground to assert your PCP. Therefore, dominance must be woven into and through all the other techniques used to make a strong first impression.

SECRET TECHNIQUES TO MAKE A STRONG FIRST IMPRESSION

The following are methods which will enable you to make a strong first impression when you meet someone new or face an unexpected situation. Developing these skills always opens the door to more techniques which you can quickly adapt for power purposes. Try them and see how you will automatically begin creating a powerful first impression every day.

But remember: people will treat you as you *expect* to be treated. This is always true on the first contact. If you step out in a bold, confident manner and immediately begin projecting yourself, you will be accorded the respect and attention due any leader.

SECRETS OF HANDLING NEW CONTACTS

If you are introduced to a new group, shake hands all around, repeat each name aloud and lean slightly toward each person as you are introduced. Use the same procedure if you introduce yourself. Then, if a topic is already under discussion, listen carefully and, at the first opportunity, add your ideas to it. Be wary of becoming embroiled in religious or political subjects since these are areas of intense opinion and can contribute little that you may turn to your benefit. If pushed for a statement, you can still show strength by clearly saying that you do not wish to comment. You should also be prepared to inject yourself into the conversation by turning it around. Do this by singling out the apparent group leader and ask him what he does, what his interests are, where he lives, etc. You may do this with each group member if time and circumstance permit. This gives you needed information to determine who you might like as a friend, and who might be most useful to you. Then, once you have established yourself in this way, you are in excellent position to guide the group into any discussion you wish because you will have made your first impression and your new friends will be eager to follow as you take charge.

On a one-to-one basis, adopt and use the same methods to take charge as you would with a new group. The effect will be equally impressive.

If you are a platform speaker, you already have an advantage since the people you are addressing take it for granted that you have the credentials to take charge. You just have to know your subject and get right into it with a forceful voice and confident authority to make a strong impression, even though there might not be one familiar face in the crowd.

• Refuse to be trapped

To make a strong first impression, refuse to be trapped. For instance, in any gathering, there are those who have little to say but say it with a motor mouth. Don't be trapped by these time-wasters. Since there is no point in worrying about a strong impression here, simply excuse yourself or just walk away from the motor mouth. Your goal is to add to your PCP. In order to accomplish that, you must operate where a strong first impression matters.

• Do the unexpected

The purpose of making a strong first impression is to place yourself where you can exercise your PCP to your benefit. One way to do this is to announce that you endorse some controversial, unpopular figure or cause which will have instant and powerful shock value. You can give credence to your statement by explaining the one or two traits you like without having to swallow the whole thing. Once you have snatched attention, you can go from there. Don't take an opposing view just to sound clever: whatever you say or do should be aimed at making a strong first impression.

The following example shows how this principle works: A minister started his first sermon to a new congregation with a choice, four-letter word. Instantly, everybody came to attention. The preacher then paused to give his technique added impetus. He then explained that he had heard the word used on the way to church, and with that, launched into a stirring sermon on the evils of profanity.

This experienced speaker appreciates the value of a strong first impression, and doing the unexpected is one of his prized secrets for accomplishing this.

● Draw your potential helper out

As you meet new people, draw out your potential helper. By doing this, you accomplish two things. First, you make a strong impression by showing an interest in a new acquaintance, and second, you bring your potential helper out into the open where you can quickly appraise him. You can do this by asking personal questions along the lines mentioned earlier, and with this done, you will know where he works, what he does best, where his interests lie, and whether he has enough power of his own to contribute anything useful to you. This strong first impression gives you the needed ammunition to apply pressure when you decide which direction your relationship with the potential helper should take. This makes the strong first impression a paying proposition.

Dan Moore met a young lady at a party and used this technique to make a power impression. In using the technique of drawing her out, he learned the lady was a knowledgeable camera enthusiast. This interested Dan since he had been using an expensive outside agency for the photography his business required. Now the potential helper he skillfully drew out at the party is on his payroll at half the cost and doing excellent work.

● Keep the ball rolling after the handshake

Remember: to make a strong first impression, keep the ball rolling after the handshake. The first impression is just that—a first impression. In order to keep the power flowing, you will need names, phone numbers, and places to contact. Gather this information and file it so that the PCP you use to make a first impression won't be lost.

It's easy to file and keep such records. B. J. Boyher, a successful industrialist, uses plain 3"×5" index cards. He carries them in a coat pocket, jots down the information on the spot, then files them under appropriate headings. When he goes back to his office, they are at his fingertips to help keep the ball rolling when he is ready to motivate, manipulate, and guide his new friends.

SECRET OF "POCKETING" PEOPLE WITH A WINNING FIRST IMPRESSION

When you "pocket" people, you have them under control. This is not because of threats or scare tactics, but rather because you have made a positive power impression upon them. The opportune time to make your positive power impression is right at the start.

The best part of making a winning impression is the long term benefits you gain. One shot deals are helpful, but it is the long-range profit in a relationship that keeps us on the top shelf. When you tie new people to you with a winning first impression, you can count on added power for about as long as you want it. These elements of a winning first impression will help you pocket people.

- Dress
- Voice
- Mannerisms
- Attitude
- Interest
- Vitality

The cut of your suit and the shine on your shoes have something to say about your power. This is not to say that you should always go around looking like a fashion plate, but dressing for the occasion is a power point in your favor. If you dress carelessly or inappropriately, you create a power stumbling block because, for whatever reason, a poor first impression is hard to overcome. Sharp dressers create a sharp impression; indifferent dressers make an indifferent impression. Which one will you make?

H. C. Lannon, senior partner in a prosperous accounting firm, refuses to even interview an applicant who is not dressed like a dedicated business man. He believes that no matter how advanced an employee's accounting knowledge may be, he is powerless to pocket a client if he isn't wise enough to dress the part.

Maybelle Elsyer considers dress a real power tool, and with reason since she manages an exclusive ladies' shop. The primary consideration in Ms. Elsyer's shop is proper dress because it gives her the extra power to "sell" customers on the first visit. Her shop's expanding clientele verifies that the winning impression ties old customers to her, and adds new ones on a daily basis.

Voice quality is also a big factor in pocketing new people. A friendly, firm tone denotes confidence and power, a harsh grating tone irritates, and a wavering voice gives the impression of weakness. But it is easy to correct negative voice habits. Talk or read into any of the inexpensive recorders available today, then play it back. Practice correcting any faults, rehearsing power speech just as if you were meeting an important person for the first time. When you can feel and hear warmth and power, you are ready to put your voice to work to tie new people to you. A practiced power voice pockets people every time.

Mannerisms are another element which ties new people to you by making a powerful impression. When your manner is reassuring, confident, and outgoing, you will attract new people. You can improve this area in much the same way that you build an effective voice. First, enlist the help of a candid friend or spouse, and ask for their suggestions. Then practice adding force to your manner while you practice eliminating any annoying habits.

Attitude is a key element with which to pocket people because it helps you make a winning impression. At the first encounter, your attitude sets up your PCP to do its job.

Keep in mind, however, that your attitude shows your mental state; it is a manner of acting, feeling, and thinking that expresses your determination, intent, and leadership. Use these thought questions to evaluate your attitude. Remember, it is for your own exclusive use, to be dwelled upon in your own mind, without even lifting a pencil. Nobody else is going to know your answers, so, be honest!

On a first contact:

(1) Do you feel and show confidence?

(2) Do you make a forceful (as opposed to forced) show of self-assurance?

(3) Are you outgoing and aggressive?

(4) Do you control the situation?

(5) Do you feel an urge to dominate?

(6) Do you relish meeting new people?

(7) Do you like to "pocket" people?

(8) Do you feel comfortable as a leader?

(9) Do you like to make the first move?

(10) Are you always looking for ways to build your people power?

If you answered "yes" to yourself as you asked these questions, then your power attitude is in good order. The power of a positive attitude is well known. It can pocket people, make more money for you, and expand your PCP instantly.

Interest and vitality, of course, are the final key ingredients in pocketing people. If you lack interest in power, people, prestige, and their benefits, you can't put much into a first impression. Vitality expresses zest and liveliness with the first contact. You can keep these two secret elements sparkling by keeping up-to-date on what interests you, by actively seeking new people to pocket, and by finding new projects for your command power. This all begins with the winning first impression you make.

THE SECRET OF GRABBING ATTENTION
TO CREATE A STRONG FIRST IMPRESSION

Grabbing attention right at the start is a potent way to make a strong impression. As an ambitious and creative personality, you will develop your own special attention-grabbing techniques as your power experience grows. You can put the following two successful methods to work now for starters.

- **Establish your qualifications first.**

When you establish your qualifications immediately, your command power is recognized at once. Having made this impression, you can make people do what you want because showing your power will convince them that you have the means and the will to get things done, and fast. The following example illustrates this strategy:

When Jeff Hursch was twenty-four and looked nineteen, he was made sales manager of the West Coast division of a national manufacturer. A sales meeting had been arranged to introduce him to the group of thirty sales agents, some of whom were men twice Jeff's age. Jeff established his qualifications with a take-charge impression when introduced by the company president.

Jeff took the mike, looked each man over coolly, then began with: "Yes, I'm the sales manager. Yes, I'm old enough to do the job. Yes, I've had enough experience to qualify me for this responsibility. Yes, I need your help and I expect it. With that out of the way, let's get to work."

Jeff grabbed attention by establishing his qualifications at the first possible moment, thus laying the groundwork for a career that has won him accolades and ever-growing PCP, which he still wields most effectively.

- **Make your point immediately.**

Making your point at once is another wonderful secret to grab attention and create a strong first impression. Mary Kimmons is a good example of how to handle this.

Mary Kimmons had been elected president of a business women's club. The club had been going downhill for several reasons: meetings had been starting late and running overtime, programs had fallen into disarray, and disorder and idle chatter had become the rule.

When Mary presided at her first meeting, she made her

point. She announced that meetings would start and end on schedule, and that speakers who ran overtime would be asked to sit down. She insisted that each member be an active, contributing part of the club which would no longer be only a place to meet and gossip. With that she banged the gavel and started the club on a most successful rebuilding program. Not surprisingly, she enjoyed nearly 100% cooperation from day one.

Often when you use a power secret to create a strong first impression, you define your qualifications, make your point, and utilize related techniques at the same time. There is no reason why you should not, because the more power you turn loose, the stronger the first impression you will make. This is added fuel for getting your way.

HOW JIM TILLMAN LANDED HIS BIGGEST DEAL BY MAKING A STRONG FIRST IMPRESSION

When Jim Tillman sat across from Fred Jefferson, the real estate expert for a huge food distributor, Jefferson had already worn out three of the town's most successful realtors. But when he was in Jim's office, Jim was ready. He had the Chamber of Commerce president on hand, along with a set of blueprints of the site he proposed to sell. He put the blueprints in front of Jefferson, and pointed out the office layout, the ample warehouse area, space for a large frozen food department, loading docks, plus a truck-servicing building. Then Jim said, "Let's go. There's only one facility like this in town. We can't risk losing it."

After the $1,000,000 deal had been closed, Mr. Jefferson confided to the Chamber of Commerce president that his strong first impression of Jim Tillman was the deciding factor in his choosing the location for his company's new branch. Indeed, Jim established his qualifications up front, and lost no time in making his point. His strong first impression had landed the biggest deal and gained him more money in one day than many men make in a year.

YOU ARE IN CHARGE WHEN YOU CREATE A STRONG FIRST IMPRESSION

It's easy to see why people respond to a strong first impression, because with this kind of power, you grab the ball. You create the instant impression that you are in charge—of yourself, of what is going on, and of everyone present. Remember this: the people whose attention you have riveted on yourself expect you to *do something about it* now that you have taken command. Don't disappoint them!

INSTANT POWER POINTERS

- The first sixty seconds is the time to make a power impression.
- People will treat you as you expect to be treated.
- Do the unexpected.
- Keep the ball rolling after the first handshake.
- A winning first impression "pockets" people.
- Attitude is a vital element in pocketing people.
- Grabbing attention is a potent way to create a strong first impression.
- Establish your qualifications promptly.
- Make your point immediately.
- People respond to a strong first impression.

8

Secrets That Develop a Winner's Attitude

There is a difference between temperament and attitude. Temperament refers to the way you habitually go about doing and saying things. Attitude is the position you take toward life and its challenges, the way you choose to regard facts and conditions, and the way you look at and how you think about reality and events that crowd in upon you each day. An attitude is also a position assumed for a specific purpose. If your temperament is easy-going and conforming, then you must harness your personal command power to reshape your mental and emotional posture for your specific purpose, which overall, is to develop an aggressive winner's attitude. Without the right attitude, nobody wins much of anything.

If you are fortunate enough to have been born with all the personality traits that go into the make-up of a winner, then your attitude is probably in fine working order. The best of us, though, need to be alert to any personality lapses that might impair our winner's attitude. This is why periodic inventories are invaluable. A winner's attitude deserves careful attention. It is the fire that keeps your PCP hot.

HOW TO ANALYZE PERSONAL POWER TRAITS

A winner's attitude deals with the positive. As a winner, your concern is to make sure that your personal power traits are developed to the fullest. The secret is to give yourself a periodic check-up. The following test can help you make a quick, mental analysis of your attitude. Give the answers that you feel apply to your particular case. You will defeat your purpose if you merely answer the questions the way you think they ought to be answered.

Are you:

   (1) Independent-minded?

   (2) Competitive?

   (3) Emotionally stable?

   (4) Persistent?

   (5) Full of staying power?

   (6) Compliant?

   (7) An introvert?

   (8) Driving?

   (9) A decision-maker?

  (10) A "nice guy" type?

  (11) Restless?

  (12) Always honest with yourself?

If your answer is yes to all these questions except numbers 6, 7, and 10, you are hitting on all cylinders. Even if you answered yes to 6, 7, or 10, there is nothing basically wrong with you, it just means that you have a bit of work to do to insure that your winner's attitude is in tip-top form. Let's examine each item briefly so that you can compare these qualities with your own attitude. This will help bring your PCP into sharp focus.

#1: Independent-minded?

Independent-mindedness indicates that you are self-reliant and sure of yourself. This is one of the basic secrets of PCP.

When you are independent-minded, you are open to ideas and suggestions, but you think for yourself and make your own decisions. There is no magic formula to obtain this trait, but it can be cultivated and developed with determination, observation, and practice.

#2: Competitive?

Being competitive means that you are not running scared. A competitor is one who accepts and meets the challenges thrown at him in business and other areas of life. Competitiveness reflects your determination to succeed, to reach your goals, and is a sign that you are willing to fight for what you want. This quality indicates that you have strengthened your PCP by putting it to daily use. This is a secret of unshakeable personal command.

#3: Emotionally stable?

This can be a disturbing question, because how do you know that you *are* emotionally stable? Consider this: an emotionally stable person is not high one day and low the next, does not panic easily nor is overly optimistic. The emotionally stable man or woman is a realist.

In severe cases of emotional instability, professional help is required. Yet it is largely a question of mind over matter: the fact that you are intent upon perfecting your PCP is a good sign that you have a grip on your emotions which, properly directed, can give sparkle and fire to your PCP.

#4: Persistent?

A winner's attitude calls for persistence. Winners don't lie down and play dead if an obstacle or two slows them down temporarily; instead, they hang in with bulldog tenacity. Persistence is another one of your secret power traits.

#5: Full of staying power?

Staying power is right next to persistence in importance. It is a combination of determination and the habit of staying with a project until you get results. It is one of the pillars of every winner's attitude.

#6: Compliant?

Everybody likes to be sweet and agreeable. Frequently, however, the cost can be too high. For instance, if you are compliant, you are bound to be pushed around a lot. Although being compliant may get you a few pats on the back, that is about all it will do for you. Don't give up your PCP just because someone wants you to. Be sweet when you can, but don't pay too much for it.

#7: Introverted?

To be introverted is to be interested in one's own mental life with a minimum of contact with other people. Obviously, this cannot be considered a power trait since PCP is an extroverted force which involves people. It logically follows, then, that to overcome this personality characteristic, one must reach out to contact and control people. This demands self-searching and a turning outward from oneself. If you use the people secrets revealed throughout this book, introversion will never be a problem for you.

#8: Driving?

A driving personality type thrives on a winner's attitude. This kind of individual is loaded with aggressiveness and fire; his winner's attitude simmers on the front burner. Mix a little drive with your winner's attitude and watch your PCP ignite.

#9: A decision-maker?

If you are a decision-maker, you have no problem with your winner's attitude because you have decided what you want and how you are going to get it. You have decided to be in charge of yourself. Your winning attitude is evident to all. They expect you to be a strong leader. This is the message the decision-maker broadcasts. Make the most of this power secret.

#10: A "nice-guy" type?

It's pleasant to be thought of as a "nice-guy" but it is too much like being compliant. It doesn't influence anybody to do anything for you. The following true story illustrates this point.

John Uhrich had just gained his first management position and a chap named Troy Coley, an outside salesman, was a member of the group John was supposed to direct. Coley was a nice guy and everybody liked him. John Uhrich was upset when he received a call within two weeks advising him to replace Troy Coley as quickly as possible. "But why?" John objected to his supervisor, "He's a nice guy. Everybody likes him!"

"Don't you know why everybody likes him; why they think he's a nice guy?" the voice on the other end of the line asked.

"Just tell me," said John, "so I'll feel better about terminating him."

"It's because he never asks his customers or anyone else to do anything for him or for his company," was the eye-opening answer.

It was a painful experience for a new manager to replace a nice guy but the point was well taken. John learned then and there that being a "nice guy" isn't always synonymous with a winner's attitude.

#11: Restless?

Good! if you are restless, it means you are not likely to be content with mediocrity. When you feel a restless urge to get things done and to manage people so they will help you attain your goals, you're on your way. It is a sure sign that you are working with a winner's attitude.

#12: Always honest with yourself?

Being honest with yourself is essential to a winner's attitude since this is how you identify your strong points and recognize personal power traits. Self-honesty isolates any deficiencies in your attitude so that you can deal with them in a hurry. It gives reason and character to your winner's attitude. Strong personalities interested in real power will never consider anything less. The fact that you are choosing self-power is evidence that honesty is important to you.

The following useful formula will help you recognize and make full use of your personal power traits to shore up your winner's attitude.

LIST YOUR POWER TRAITS—LIST YOUR GOALS

It is a colossal waste to build power for the sake of power. To be worth anything, PCP must be used for positive purposes. Of course, in this materialistic world it makes sense that you should use it to get what you want. Anything less would be a disservice to yourself and to those who rely and depend upon you.

Very few individuals make full use of all the PCP that they possess. In fact, many are surprised at the great reserves of power at their disposal once they begin researching and studying PCP and its varied applications. Try this exercise as an example: make two lists on opposite sides of a separate sheet of paper. Head one side "Power traits" and the other side "Goals." Make the lists as long and inclusive as you like. Use the following as an illustration.

My Power Traits	My Goals
Independence	Power
Studiousness	Education
Hard working	Success
Reliability	Recognition
Imaginativeness	Love
Trustworthiness	Respect
Aggressiveness	Prestige
Strong Vocal Ability	Family
Competitiveness	Home
Persistence	Management
Determination	Responsibility
Observation	Travel
Ambition	Security
Objectivity	Leadership
Realism	Money
Enterprising	Service

Now, put everything that comes to mind on your lists. Remember, it is especially important that you put every possible PCP trait under "My Power Traits." The lists need not be the same length.

After you have completed your lists, compare them. You will be amazed at the number of power traits at your finger tips and where they can take you. Don't neglect a single one; instead, sharpen them and put them to work. When you do, you will be able to reach every goal on your other list.

EMPHASIZE YOUR POWER TRAITS

The secret to developing a fiery, dominating attitude is this: put the emphasis on your power traits. This keeps your winner's attitude on the positive side. Don't weaken your resources with pointless self-recrimination. You do not have to be the embodiment of perfection in order to develop a winner's attitude. It is enough to perfect and utilize the power traits you already have.

DON'T BLOW UP MINOR WEAKNESSES

With a winner's attitude, it is easy to excuse the weaknesses and minor defects in those around you. But should you be *less* charitable to yourself? Yes, because PCP is at stake. It is vital that you recognize your weak spots, for how else can you get them out in the open and deal with them? The secret is to consistently work to eliminate or strengthen them. However, it is destructive to exaggerate minor weak points in your personality until they overshadow and hide your vast untapped power elements. Instead, deal with them realistically—as you must—but remember your power traits are what count.

You can keep your weak points in perspective. First isolate them one by one. Then use the self-discipline that is a major ingredient to your PCP to rid yourself of them.

HOW JOE BARTLE WHIPPED A WEAK POINT

Joe Bartle was sensitive to the point of being vacillating. When business was down in his department of the chemical manufacturing plant where he worked, the board of directors had heaped unreasonable restrictions on his department. Advertising had been curtailed, salesmen's compensation had been reduced, and research was practically nil. Joe disliked confrontation and fireworks, but soul searching revealed plainly to him that he was acting too benignly. The next time Joe was called on the carpet, he shed his weakness with a show of power. He stood tall, faced the management team and explained that he could no longer accept their incorrect analysis of either the company's problems or his performance. He told them that it was the board's action that had created the downturn, that the board had stopped needed research, had reduced advertising to the point of no return, and had created dissatisfaction and turnover in the sales force. He concluded by stating he was ready to do his part, but he could no longer stand by and accept condemnation for the mistakes of others.

With this, Joe turned his company around by putting his new-found winner's attitude to work. It worked for Joe; it will work for you.

SECRETS THAT MAKE THE MOST OF YOUR WINNER'S ATTITUDE

You invariably reap the results of your own attitude. If your attitude is weak, what you get from it will be weak; if your attitude is positive and power-filled, you will get powerful results. Make the most of this truth by utilizing the following helpful ideas.

● Keep your self-image sound

Your power begins when you accept the fact that you have the resources to make decisions, to dominate, and to control. The acceptance of this reality gives you self-respect that is solid as a rock because your self-image says you are a winner. If you do not accept and believe this power secret, how can anybody else? What you think of yourself is what other people will think of you. How you act toward yourself is how others will act toward you. Wherever you lead they will follow. Emblazon this in your mind: when you get out of bed every morning, your self-image is going to determine how the day goes for you.

● Spotlight your winner's attitude on a specific goal

If you scatter your power in too many directions, you will become ineffective. Give your goals priority. Go after them one at a time. As you reach one goal, your exhilarating sense of accomplishment will add to your winning attitude. Consequently, each goal becomes easier than the last. If you try to do too much, you could end up with Ryan Cosby's problems.

Ryan, who had just passed his bar examination, was ambitious, informed, and determined to be a winner. As soon as he hung up his shingle, he joined a church, a civic club, the Chamber of Commerce, and a country club. He accepted the chairmanship of two major charity drives, took over the presidency of a professional fraternity, and made speeches every time he was asked. As a result, he was going to bed exhausted every night and waking up confused every morning. Soon his law practice dropped off. He had the winner's attitude, but it was being fragmented and spread too thin. When Mr. Cosby came to this realization, he began restricting his outside activities to reasonable limits and pointed his winner's attitude at his law practice once again. Now, this respected attorney is still generous with his time, but not at the expense of his practice. His PCP keeps his winner's attitude focused on his main goal, as it should be.

● Direct your winner's attitude at those who have something to offer

Point your winner's attitude only at those people who have something to offer you. There is nothing to be gained in dominating and influencing chronic losers. It's all right to help them, however, if you expect no more than the personal satisfaction that comes from a charitable act. Deal with those people who are in a position to help you get what you want.

● Use your winner's attitude as a control technique

A winner's attitude is a control technique because to begin with, it takes personal control to develop and maintain a strong, winner's attitude. And once you have a winner's attitude, you make the most of it by using it to control your life, influence other lives, and control where you are going. The key is that *all* the power to control your winner's attitude is yours alone and *all* the power that just naturally emanates from your winner's attitude belongs to you exclusively.

True, attitude is an abstract quality, but you can use the secret techniques that we have covered to give your attitude muscle, bone, and fiber. As you develop your winner's attitude with these power secrets, your PCP explodes right along with your winner's attitude.

INSTANT POWER POINTERS

- There is a difference between temperament and attitude.
- A winner's attitude deals with the positive.
- Give yourself a power-trait check-up periodically.
- List your power traits, then list your goals.
- Emphasize your power traits.
- Don't blow-up your own weaknesses.
- Spotlight your winner's attitude on special goals.
- Direct your attitude at those who have something to offer you.
- Your winner's attitude is a control technique.

9

Command Secrets That Build
Self-Confidence

A succinct definition of self-confidence is "confidence in oneself and in one's powers and abilities." We could very well have said "confidence in oneself and confidence in one's personal command power." It amounts to the same thing, because in dealing with PCP the emphasis is on self-confidence.

Self-confidence is worthy of close study. It is the priceless ingredient that keeps you off the psychiatrist's couch and in the arena of life. It is the secret of doers; the launch pad of your "powers and abilities."

HOW TO CLAIM YOUR RIGHT TO SELF-CONFIDENCE

Do you have a right to self-confidence? Have you earned that right? The answer is an unqualified yes. When you stood up as a toddler and took your first step, you claimed your right to self-confidence. If this right has been weakened or laid aside temporarily, you can pick it up because you earned it with that first wobbly step. The only one who can deny you that right is you.

If you feel that your self-confidence is racked by an inferiority complex, try making up your mind that you are not a powerless blob floating around in an overwhelming environment. Not a big percentage of us ever feel the need for psychiatric counselling since most people can recognize their inferiority symptoms. The remedy is to turn your personal powers and abilities loose on any of your confidence-robbing faults.

Young Sid Haas had taken his first job as a sporting goods salesman for Big Frost Sporting Goods, Inc. Because of his short stature, Sid was the butt of a lot of good-natured jokes from his athletic and sports-minded customers. He felt a sense of inadequacy pressing in upon him. And it was hard for him to feel the equal of the physical types that his work naturally threw him with every day. Sid possessed normal intelligence, a desire to excel, and wanted to belong. He put his PCP to work. Sid soon became an authority on every piece of sports equipment. More, he studied prominent athletes until he could talk with enthusiasm and authority about them. He pored over sports records, statistics, rules, and history until he was a walking sports encyclopedia. Soon he was in much demand as a speaker, and became the final word on any sports subject. His sales also climbed steadily, and his friends included big name sports figures. Now when they called him "Shorty," he recognized it as an affectionate term which no longer gave him pangs of inferiority. Sid had built his self-confidence to the point where he knew that he had the respect of his peers. He had proven to everyone that he had the power and ability to not only cope, but to win. He believed in himself, which is the secret ingredient of self-confidence. It is also a not-so-secret ingredient in personal command power.

SECRETS TO WHIP EXCUSES OF INFERIORITY

Well-meaning behavioral experts have supplied us with many excuses for inadequacy and failure. We can just about pick and choose if we are looking for an excuse for having an inferiority complex. However, a closer look at these power-robbers will reveal their true nature and lack of validity. Consider the following factors.

• A lack of education need not be fatal

A lack of extensive formal education is often cited as an excuse for a galling sense of inferiority. Formal education is wonderful, but it is not the only valuable thing in life, nor is it the only criteria for power, ability, and success. Our country has had more than one president who lacked a college education.

If you are bothered by a lack of formal education, all is not lost. You can acquire the knowledge and culture that you would get in college by reading. Read often and on many subjects. Also, more and more adults are attending evening classes at universities and colleges across the land. I myself have spent considerable time in such classes. This is an admirable way to refresh your thinking, increase your general knowledge, gain new skills, and keep up-to-date. I can vouch that this is a great way to overcome any lack of educational self-confidence.

• About aptitude tests

Suppose you have taken an aptitude test that didn't turn out as well as you hoped. So what? Don't let this affect your self-confidence. These things are relative and do not measure all the qualities that go into PCP. For one, I have never seen a test that could accurately predict how hard a man would work for success. Nor do I believe that there is one yet devised that will measure anyone's willingness to work as much, or as long as a project might demand. Further, you can develop, improve, and raise your intelligence quotient, and for what it is worth, recall what an intelligence quotient is: "a number used to express the *apparent* relative intelligence of a person determined by dividing his mental age, as reported on a standardized test, by his chronological age and multiplying by 100."

• How to put a deprived childhood behind you

A deprived childhood is an old favorite when it comes to excuses used to explain or justify a crippling inferiority complex. An unhappy, underprivileged childhood is regrettable. Yet history books are full of leaders who suffered tragic childhoods. Scores of today's business leaders endured poverty-ridden youth. No doubt you know some successful people who were once neglected as children. A man I know has operated a popular, profitable restaurant for years because he was often hungry as a child. The best school teacher I ever had sawed timber and drove mules with semi-literate companions as a boy. The accomplishments of tens of thousands of men and women, who exercised PCP to put a deprived childhood behind them, is mute testimony that this is not a valid reason for feeling inferior. Whatever your childhood, you can claim the self-confidence that is yours by right. Put your childhood behind you, where it belongs.

● **How to make it without a breezy manner**

There are those who show concern because they do not have a breezy manner or glib tongue. Do not think of these as cause for suggesting an inferiority complex. The truth is that these two personality traits can actually irritate. For example, two recent college graduates, Lori Wright and Kim Little, were being interviewed for a supervisory position in the administrative office of a huge city hospital. Lori was breezy and talkative, while Kim was polite and reserved. The girls were equally qualified, but Kim got the job because Lori's breezy and talkative attitude was considered inappropriate for the position.

Be dependable, strong and determined. This is more important than a breezy manner and a quick, glib tongue.

● **Avoid suicidal behavior**

Don't indulge in suicidal behavior by succumbing to a feeling of inferiority. Instead, use the secrets and techniques available to you to whip any inferiority excuses. No punishment is as destructive as self-inflicted punishment, no waste is more tragic than neglected PCP.

HOW TO FACE MAJOR SITUATIONS WITH SELF-CONFIDENCE

At a recent college graduation, a speaker with a doctorate in psychology told the graduates that there are three major situations in life that they would face: the known, the unknown and the haphazard. The doctor went on to explain that among the best things that schools could teach students which would equip them to meet these situations was self-confidence. This thesis supports our study of command secrets and techniques that build self-confidence.

HOW TO FACE THE KNOWN WITH SELF-CONFIDENCE

Some things we know are going to happen every day. There will be economic demands, pressures, schedules, competition, decisions and on and on. There is no way to escape the predictable, even if we drop out of productive society since we wind up inheriting a different set of problems which are degrading and demeaning. There is no point jumping from the frying pan into the fire.

It may seem incredulous, but the recognizable, daily expected events are what cause the most problems. Worry and fretting over what we know will happen, who we know we will face, and what we know is expected of us undermines self-confidence in many otherwise rational, intelligent people.

Dan Carney was promoted from sales manager to executive vice-president of a multi-operational electronics company. His track record as sales manager was impressive, to say the least, his educational attainments in marketing and business administration were outstanding. He had every reason to tackle his new job with self-confidence. He knew full well what was expected, what he had to do and who he had to deal with on an ongoing basis, yet he worried and stewed so much each night that he dreaded the next day. Within two months, he sought professional help. A competent psychologist quickly put Mr. Carney back on track. Today he is handling his executive position with enthusiasm and remarkable effectiveness. He has trouble explaining why he abandoned his customary self-confidence for a while, but he has agreed to share his secrets for meeting the known factors of business life with success and confidence. Of course, the same secrets work in personal life as well, so consider these points Dan Carney endorses.

- **Secrets to handle known situations with confiden**

  1. *Map your strategy.*

     Since you know what's likely to happen, you can map your strategy. You won't have to diagram every move and then operate by rote. Remain a bit flexible and use your PCP to make things happen as you want them to happen. Then, expect the best possible results. Planning plus the determined use of self-confidence will give you the power to handle any opposition.

  2. *Train your mind not to worry.*

     Yes, you can train your mind not to worry. When you have decided on a plan, think of what you are going to make happen. If worry or doubt tries to encroach, close your eyes and blot it all out by mentally rehearsing your plans. Sticking with the positive aspects of known facts erases worry and builds your self-confidence.

  3. *Feel good about what you can do.*

     When you face the known, take inventory of yourself. This will make you feel good about what you are able to do: it gives you the right to face the known with confidence to spare.

- **Secrets to face the unknown and the haphazard**

  Your capacity to face the unknown and the haphazard (which, for practical purposes, is the same thing) will depend largely on the attitude you choose for yourself. In fact, *self-confidence is an attitude.* You can choose it or reclaim it much as we have just discussed in the Dan Carney case. You do not have to be a victim for anybody. The secret is to use your PCP and recognize that you can control your attitude toward any situation.

  Jess Hall wanted to know what was going to happen to him every minute of every day. He insisted on strict routine in both his office and his home. He was angered by and frightened of the unknown and haphazard areas of his business and personal life. It took two years and thousands of dollars of psychiatric counselling before Jess was convinced that he could control his attitude. He later admitted that he had wanted to find deep-rooted psychological explanations for his unreasonable dread of the unknown, but fortunately for Jess, he saw that his problem wasn't all that complicated. He simply readjusted his attitude and now faces challenging situations with reasonable confidence.

HOW TO REPLACE SELF-DOUBT WITH SELF-CONFIDENCE

Self-doubt is self-destruction. If you feel an occasional twinge of self-doubt, there are simple and effective ways to wipe it out. You are the one who must choose self-confidence over self-doubt. The following points are ideas that you can use today to replace any self-doubts with self-confidence.

● Cultivate a healthy self-image

If you doubt that you are smart, you will only encourage the people whom you should be controlling to question your intelligence. If you doubt that you can do a job, your associates will join you in your misgivings. If you doubt that you can be an effective leader, then the people who should be following you will also doubt you can be a leader.

Larry Keene, six feet and two inches tall, nursed a sorry image of himself for two years after graduating from college. He had prepared to work as a fashion illustrator, but the field was overcrowded. As a result, he took a job in an office where he was thoroughly miserable. He was depressed, felt that he was a failure, and his self-image was low, low, low. Then, as Larry likes to say, he "screwed his head back on." He took personal inventory and decided he had something to offer after all. He made up a dynamic new resumé aptly illustrated with his own work, and within three weeks was working for an aggressive advertising agency. Mr. Keene had the qualifications to land a good job all along, but he didn't take advantage of his power until he developed a healthy self-image. A strong self-image is a fantastic secret to use in building your self-confidence.

● Don't join the self-punishers

The business and professional worlds and the social community all have more than enough self-punishers. These are the misfits who hide behind every imaginable excuse to justify a dismal lack of self-confidence. You recognize them every day. Stay away from them. The affliction is highly contagious.

● Avoid explaining everything you do

Don't explain everything that you do to anybody. Otherwise you will soon begin talking to yourself. And that's no way to replace self-doubt with self-confidence.

● Your first responsibility is to you

When I was very young, I was fortunate enough to know a philanthropic businessman. I expressed my admiration for the big-hearted gifts he gave to institutions and needy individuals. I asked him how he did it. He told me it required much self-discipline, but that you'll never get in trouble as long as you remember: *your first responsibility is to you.*

That makes good sense, doesn't it? How can you set examples and lead people until you fulfill your obligation to yourself? But here is a bonus; when you fulfill your obligation to yourself, you build self-confidence. Remember that, too.

SECRETS TO PUT SELF-CONFIDENCE TO WORK TODAY

Self-confidence, like all power secrets, is meaningless until you use it to get what you need from people. Self-confidence is a people-proposition. This is where it is put to the test, where it is of great value to you in dealing with people. Only by directing (using) other strong characters can you reach your maximum potential. Self-confidence, controlled and cemented into your own personality, is an absolute necessity.

Here are some ideas that you can use to put your self-confidence to work, today.

(1) Make a personal asset chart

List every good thing about yourself on a separate sheet of paper. You will soon be surprised at how much you have going for yourself.

Check over these to help you start your chart.

Ambition	Education	Health
Desire	Experience	Mobility
Stability	Foresight	Organizational Ability
Determination	Goals	Mix well
Fearlessness	Risk Taking	Entrepreneurial talent
Enterprising	Neatness	Conscientiousness
Hobbies	Training	Talent

These are only a *few* of the power assets the normal individual can tap. Even so, they often are not associated with self-confidence. Fill a page or two with your assets and fit all these elements into your self-confidence attitude. They will work for you today, tomorrow, and the next day.

(2) Give a star to key people

Write down the names of the people around you. This can be used as your own people-resource. Put a star by the names of the people you want to use in order to further your goals. For example, if you want a promotion, put a star by the name of the person you should use to achieve that goal. If you want a transfer, make the star and go to work on the party who can help you get it. And, if a project is as simple as finding a desirable date, put a star by the name of whomever you like and take that person to dinner. Making a list of people around you and noting how you can use them beneficially gives focus to your self-confidence. The better placed your stars, the more your self-confidence will do for you.

(3) Label yourself A #1 today

Of course you want to improve as you move ahead. You plan to work at becoming more and more proficient at using people power to get what you want. The thought is exciting, but, as you can see after making your personal assets chart, you have plenty going for you *today*. Label yourself A #1, and put self-confidence to work now. You will be astonished at how quickly people will respond to you. Then, as you garner more experience in using self-confidence to get people to do what you want, your goals and achievements will progressively expand to ever greater proportions.

Farris Craigmore, a friend of mine, had $500 and a second-hand truck thirty years ago. But then he labeled himself A #1, put the money he had into a small stock of merchandise, and hit the road. Today Mr. Craigmore heads a major distribution firm which is totally computerized, with over one hundred employees. He has a stable of show horses, farms, investments, is an alderman, and is on his bank's as well as a national corporation's board of directors. This community leader has many active years and ever bigger plans ahead.

Craigmore believes in self-confidence which he likes to call "guts." Call it what you will, but as this gentleman says, "it will take you as far as you want to go." Label yourself A #1 as Mr. Craigmore did, and put your self-confidence to work!

INSTANT POWER POINTERS

- You have a right to self-confidence.
- Feel good about what you can do.
- Self-confidence can handle big situations.
- Self-doubt is self-destruction.
- Your first responsibility is to yourself.
- Cultivate a healthy self-image.
- Don't join the self-punishers.
- You don't have to explain everything you do.
- Self-confidence means nothing until it's put into action.
- Self-confidence involves people.
- Label yourself A #1.

10

Personal Command Power
= People Power

Personal command power is people power: that is absolute. People power is the personal ability to motivate, control, use, guide, direct, and influence the people around you. This means you must move people to do what you want them to do.

Most of the self-improvement books I have read have emphasized how hard you should work to help other people get what *they* want. This, of course is in the vague hope that they, in turn, will be ready to help you get what you want. Well, that is very nice, but not quite the way it works most of the time. How many favors have you had returned lately?

Granted, the ideal is to help others as we lead them into helping us. Aside from this altruistic philosophy, PCP is basically a tool to help you get what you want through the judicious use of people. If you can help others attain their goals in the bargain, that is a commendable fringe benefit. This is basic: people power—personal command power—is designed, intended, and should be programmed, to move people to help you get what you want. Do not squander it.

Before we wind up this introductory discussion on the relative merits of PCP and its logical use, here is an observation

112

made well over 1000 years ago by the Greek historian Dionysius
of Halicarnassus:

> "It is a law of nature, common to all mankind, which
> time shall neither annul nor destroy, that those who have
> greater strength and power shall bear rule over those who
> have less."

So far, no one has proved Dionysius wrong.

PEOPLE ARE THE FACTOR

For our purpose, a factor is "something that actively con-
tributes to the production of a result." The result is the goal you
aim for. People are the factor that will help you get what you
want. They are the only factor that you can use to expand and
explode your power, so every technique, every idea in this book
is presented to enable you to take full advantage of the people
factor.

POWER TECHNIQUES TO MOTIVATE
PEOPLE YOUR WAY

An ambitious man or woman who lacks the skill and drive
to motivate and lead people is about as helpless as a one-legged
duck. The ideas and techniques that follow can insure that you
will never be in such hapless condition.

• Use excitement

Action excites. When you start a project, give your helpers
just a glimpse of what is in store. As you do so, make your own
action visible. When people see that you are excited enough to
be actively involved in your ideas and projects, they will get
excited and jump right in with you. This is aptly illustrated in
Dennis Morrisett's story.

Dennis recently had a great idea: he created a time-saving
research service for banks of all sizes. His next step was to have
an advertising agency draw up illustrations and charts, which

made a terrific presentation. Then, because it all looked so simple and saleable, he hired three sales people and sent them out with his red hot idea and beautiful sales aids. Nothing happened. Dennis called a meeting. He excitedly went back and gave each salesman another glimpse of the big potential his idea and his service represented. Next, he went into action by making enthusiastic calls with each of his men. Within two weeks, he had fifty new subscribers at $300 per month. Today he has a multi-state operation of his own and is busily franchising in other states. In this case, a little excitement and action launched a rewarding idea for Dennis Morrisett. It will do as much for you because excitement and action will invariably motivate people your way.

● **Give your helpers a feeling of power**

Everybody wants power in one form or another. There is plenty to go around. As you motivate and use people, you can give them a feeling of power. The beauty of this is that it will not diminish or weaken your power over them. This point is illustrated by a tragic case history I witnessed.

Ed Jetmore clawed and fought his way into a sales manager's job. After he finally made it, he tried to do everything himself. No decision was so trivial that he did not insist on being the final authority. He humiliated intelligent men by his demeaning arrogance. Sales slipped and salesmen left. His department was a shambles until a new manager was brought in. He redeveloped the sales program, rehired many of the men Jetmore had run off, and sought strong men to replace those who refused to come back. He gave each man clearly defined responsibility and the leeway to act. Immediately, sales shot upward as each man on the sales force was imbued with a feeling of power and independence, yet all the while the new sales manager held tight rein. He knew he needed people to make his own power grow; furthermore, he knew that giving his men a feeling of their own power would make them work harder for him.

However and wherever you apply your PCP, you should not avoid giving your helpers a bit of self-power. When you give them their own taste of power, they will put it to work for you as long as you set the pace and keep them moving your way.

HOW TO LINE PEOPLE UP YOUR WAY

When you line people up your way, you are building people power for a purpose. You are programming them to do something the way that you want it done. One way or the other, when you line people up your way, you must instruct them to do something. The way you express your order will determine how quickly you will line up your helpers. The next section will give you some helpful ideas.

● How to issue an obvious order

Do not weaken an obvious order with such polite and well-intentioned expressions such as "let's," "perhaps," and "please." Anything but a direct order weakens the authority of your command. The following examples will dramatically illustrate how such phrases can take the teeth out of an order.

1. "Meet here at 8 o'clock tomorrow morning."
1a. "Let's meet here at 8 o'clock tomorrow morning."
2. "Make 10 calls today."
2a. "See if you can't make 10 calls today."
3. "This unit will sell at $50 net."
3a. "Perhaps this unit will sell at $50 net."
4. "Get this order out today."
4a. "Please get this order out today."
5. "Put this in the mail today."
5a. "Don't you think this should get in the mail today?"

There is no point in being unnecessarily belligerent when you give an order, but there is no excuse for weakening an order with words that invite questions and inaction. You are the decision maker when you issue an order. Don't weaken your orders with unsure statements that invite your helpers to dilute your decisions. Don't leave the door open for action-delaying questions. Giving clear orders will help line your people up your way.

Now go down the list again and read each statement aloud. Which sounds more authoritative? Which would you respond to more quickly? Which conveys more power?

In every case, the first expression is the power expression containing an obvious order that demands immediate action. The sense of power comes through loud and clear in the leading command, while the "a" examples are diluted and flabby.

● Never say anything you don't mean

When you are trying to line people up your way, do not make the mistake of saying anything you do not intend to act upon. If you make a threat and chicken out, you are dead. If you make a firm promise and fail to keep it, the helpers you propose to line up will walk away. Stick to things you can carry out, and promise only what you know you can deliver. Operating on this basis will keep your PCP solid, and it will keep your people in line.

● What to do when your people drag their feet

Sometimes you may find it necessary to violate the dictates of your usually sweet and reasonable personality. This can happen when you have formulated a project, selected the people you plan to use, and issued detailed instructions, only to find that your helpers seem trapped in the doldrums. In such cases, a little shock treatment may be in order. Dillon Mason puts it this way, "You may have to try a bit of plain and fancy whiplashing." Here's an account of how Mr. Mason laid it on in style on one occasion.

Dillon Mason is a distributor for a well-known food supplement and household item franchise group. Each Monday morning there was a sales meeting which lasted only an hour, but by noon Mason was still trying to shoo the hangers-on away from the coffee machine. Conviviality was rampant, but sales left something to be desired. Mr. Mason knew that the time for action had come. At the next Monday meeting, he pulled the plug on the coffeemaker and announced that anybody who didn't get out and make their quota for the week would be summarily dismissed. All except two talkative ladies made their quota, and Mr. Mason, good as his word, terminated them on the spot. Since then, sales have improved remarkably while coffee consumption has declined noticeably.

Had Dillon Mason welched on his threat to fire the non-producers, what would have happened? He would have lost control and his business would have continued to deteriorate. Mr. Mason exercised his PCP and put his helpers to work. That's what PCP is about.

Other shock treatments that you can use on the laggards are these: withholding expected favors, replacing deadwood, dramatically selecting new key people, openly kicking out troublemakers, and generally acting like the man in charge. Shocking action may be a last resort, but it is a power technique. Use it if your people show an inclination to drag their feet.

HOW TO AVOID A GUILT TRIP
AS YOU TURN ON PEOPLE POWER

It is a favorite trick of whiners and losers to try making strong personalities feel guilty. Unfortunately, this under-handed ploy (which is really what it is meant to be by the sanctimonious complainer) has been known to work against an unsuspecting victim. Strong people can also be sensitive indi-viduals. It is a mistake, nevertheless, to be trapped into giving in to such a deceptive appeal. This would be abandoning your people power without rhyme or reason.

You can avoid taking a guilt trip by seeing a complaint or weak, plaintive appeal for what it is; a sly unscrupulous attempt to undermine your power and put you on the defensive.

One sensible, determined young lady handled one of these annoying and troublesome plotters with authority. She was a brilliant executive in the business community, but she had a demanding, self-centered mother. The mother made her daugh-ter's life miserable by phoning day and night, complaining that nobody had time for her or showed her love and appreciation anymore. Why, oh why, couldn't her own daughter drop everything and run little errands for her loving old mother? She really knew how to lather on the guilt!

The daughter stopped these killer tactics cold by writing her mother a brief note. She explained quite simply that she did indeed love her mother, but that she could not and would not permit her to continue interfering with her business or meddle in her affairs. She further stated that she would no longer accept phone calls or stop by every evening just to pacify her mother. She closed by asking that her mother write her a note as soon as she was ready to reestablish their relationship on a more wholesome basis. (Remember, she wasn't taking phone calls from Mama.)

Within two weeks she had her reply: well-written, apologetic, and conciliatory. You can bet that both women are much happier because the daughter resolutely rejected a guilt trip.

Chronic complainers are often self-righteous souls who try to steal power by making their victims feel guilty. One veteran salesman had a new customer who was a chronic complainer. He subconsciously tried to plaster guilt on the suppliers and salesmen who called on him by harping that service was rotten, that the big boys made all the money anyway, and that salesmen got fat on whopping commissions. After listening to this tale of woe two or three times, the salesman asked, "Sir, did you get this store and make all your money by trying to make people feel that they were no good? That seems to be your total attitude these days. I cannot accept that."

The store owner, of course, protested that the salesman was wrong. But he did stop his chronic downgrading and complaining, which was keen evidence that the salesman had hit the mark by refusing to go on a guilt trip.

There can be no winners when anybody takes a guilt trip. One person will lose his PCP, and the other will lose his or her self-respect, because he or she will keep working the beggar's trick of laying guilt on weak-hearted victims. This is another reason not to be swayed from your campaign to build more and more people power for yourself.

To avoid a costly guilt trip, try these extra secrets.

1. Turn the tables on the guilt peddler

For every situation in which some misguided loser is trying to apply the guilt, there are effective ways to put the shoe on the other foot. The guilt peddler tries to play on your sympathy to bring you under his control by alternately scolding, praising, whimpering, cajoling, coaxing, or threatening. Don't be bamboozled; the shoe will soon be on the other foot if you don't budge from your avowed position. Express no sympathy or pity, for, if you do, the guilt peddler will try to use it as a wedge to get you to knuckle under and yield your power to him. Be objective and stick to your guns. You will be surprised at how quickly the guilt peddler will come over to your side.

2. Remember that guilt power is false power

Guilt is a shadowy, sick emotion on which to build power. It usually has no basis in truth. It depends solely on assaulting the victim's sense of fair play to cause a breakdown through self-condemnation. It seeks to pull the strong down in order to gain an unearned advantage. See it for what it is: false power.

3. Keep a tight control on your emotions

When an opponent is trying to destroy or weaken your people power by using guilt, he is usually pretty coy about it. He tries to trick you into an emotional surrender while pleading his own self-demeaning frustration. The thinly disguised implication here is that you are heartless, cruel, stupid, unfeeling, and inconsiderate if you will not lie down and play dead for this deceptive individual. You can avoid this guilt trip by keeping a steady grip on your emotions. Remember: you know the merit of your position and you know that your own power is backed by your convictions and ambition. It needs no apology. Stifle any attack on your emotional state by refusing to give credence to the dramatics, the inflated anger, the offended stance, or the crocodile tears of the guilt peddler.

4. Use people power as offense power

People power is more than a defense mechanism even though it is highly effective in this area. But it is primarily an offensive power which indicates that you can expect some keen opposition as you apply your PCP. Herein lies one of the elementary prerequisites of people power, i.e., that you apply it offensively to outmaneuver, outwit, and overcome opposition. This is the only logical way to deal with the nefarious opponent who whines and complains as he tries to make you feel guilty. When you apply your PCP in this manner, you will avoid any guilt trips while you let loose your people power.

TAKE ADVANTAGE OF THIS FACT: PEOPLE WANT TO BE BOSSED

If everybody were a boss, nobody would be the boss. It would be a sorry and confusing state. People want to be bossed. The average person wants and needs a strong leader, just as a nation wants and needs a strong leader. When you are the boss, you are the leader; when you apply PCP, you are the boss. Take advantage of the fact that people want to be bossed.

There are a multitude of explanations as to why most people would rather be bossed than boss. Dispensing with the psychological and sociological theories, here are some reasons for this attitude that both you and I have observed.

1. It is hard work to be the boss

It is not easy to be the boss because you have to make the rules, enforce them, and set the pace. You have to use power, which can be exhausting. As the boss, you must initiate, imagine, and plan, and be able to ignore the clock. This is all hard work, and it is also the reason you are, or will be, the boss. You want to be the chief instead of one of the faceless Indians. You have the PCP, the discipline, and the people power to be boss. Even so, it is still difficult. But it is also rewarding and exciting. You can be glad that bossing is hard work. This fact leaves the field wide open for those of you who are willing to make the most of your people power.

2. Being boss demands responsibility

As boss, you are responsible for getting projects done, for using people constructively, and for motivating others to do what you want. Most people don't want that much responsibility. Most people also forego a great percentage of their PCP. The man who uses people power to get what he wants, reach his goals, and raise the sights of his fellow man, fulfills a great responsibility to himself and others. Most people do not wish to assume such a great responsibility and would rather be bossed. And they want *you* to use your people power.

Jess Whitaker wanted to be one of the boys, even after he was made plant manager at Carroll Coatings Incorporated. He acted like one of the boys until the board of directors demanded an explanation for the decreased productivity since Jess became manager. Knowing his job was in jeopardy, especially in view of the fact that he had no logical explanation for the declining productivity, Jess reexamined his thinking. Without realizing it, he used people power by giving definite assignments, setting quotas, and issuing clear-cut orders. The results amazed Mr. Whitaker as production doubled and employee morale improved. He had made a startling discovery: being boss demands personal responsibility. This discovery, he says today, is the big secret than enabled him to become president of Carroll Coatings Incorporated today.

Consider these two thoughts and you too will move ahead just as Jess Whitaker did. (1) Being boss demands responsibility. (2) Most people don't aspire to that much responsibility.

True, it is hard work being the boss; yes, it demands personal responsibility. But, people want to be bossed, and the man or woman who skillfully uses people power can be the boss. The rewards are enormous.

INSTANT POWER POINTERS

- Personal command power is people power.
- Power is a tool to help you get what you want.
- People are the factor.
- Power techniques motivate people your way.
- Lining people up your way builds power.
- Use the whip-lash technique when you must.

- Beware of the guilt trip.
- Turn the tables on the guilt peddler.
- People want to be bossed.
- You can be the boss.
- The rewards are enormous.

11

Power Secrets That Win Respect

Respect, like love, cannot be demanded. It must be commanded. Therefore, it logically follows that the more wisely and effectively you use your personal command power, the more respect you can win. It is essential to remember that PCP is a waste unless it is used to attain a constructive goal; it is too valuable to be thrown away in blustery, pointless outbursts. But, when used to win respect, it is of inestimable value and is a power secret that you can use to your advantage.

A LAW OF HUMAN NATURE
THAT YOU CAN USE TO GENERATE RESPECT

There is an indisputable law that it's human nature to respect forceful personalities.

Think about that. How many people do you know who have pussyfooted their way to respect? In history books and on the street where you live, it is the strong personality who commands respect. A simple example of how this law works follows.

Stan Eisman was making his first call on La-Chem, Inc., an old customer of his firm. This account, a large wood product manufacturer, had habitually ordered 10 barrels of contact adhesive each trip. On Stan's first call, his sales manager who had accompanied Stan by way of introduction, saw a concrete demonstration of how a forceful personality can skillfully apply power to win respect and the accompanying benefits. Stan confidently insisted that his customer should buy a truckload of 100 barrels. He forcefully explained the advantages of such an order as opposed to the piece-meal orders the firm had traditionally given a less aggressive salesman. After Stan had made his strong presentation, Harry Marcine, the sales manager, heard the purchasing agent say, "Yeah, I think we can handle that okay, Mr. Eisman."

With a keen application of the law that human nature respects forceful personalities, Stan Eisman earned the respect of his buyer and his boss.

This law of human nature works equally well in those small, annoying situations as it does in the bigger, more important matters. For instance, recently I was checking into a motel in Arkansas that was one of an international group which prides itself on courtesy and helpfulness. But when I asked the receptionist to make a reservation for me for the next leg of my trip, she scribbled a number on her scratch pad and said, "Here's the number. You can call it yourself from the lobby phone." I placed my preferred customer card back down on the counter and said, "I expect you to use your direct line and do it for me. That will save me the hassle of doing it the hard way, and it will save me the trouble of explaining to your company's president that you are not in agreement with his spirit of being helpful and courteous to paying guests."

In exactly two minutes, I had my confirmed reservation and an apology from the insolent receptionist and the inn manager.

There is no respect or pleasure gained in being crude and brutish, and there is even less gotten from being servile and obsequious. When you use your power secrets with firm resolve, no one is going to regard you as a fluttery butterfly with stained glass wings. Instead, they will understand that you are in dead earnest, and they will respect you for it.

To take full advantage of this law of human nature, impress

these points on your mind as you use your power secrets to win respect:

- Use tactful force promptly:
  Later can be much too late.
- Keep cool:
  Shoo the butterflies out of sight.
- Sound and act as if you expect respect and cooperation.
  This insures that you will win what you want.
- Keep the pressure on until your goal is achieved.
  This will guarantee that you earn respect and complete your project.

HOW TO USE LEADERSHIP TO WIN RESPECT

Leaders are the people others listen to and follow. Leadership is the ability to make people listen to you, follow you and respect you in the process. Use the following techniques of leadership to win respect:

- **Exert authority**

Effective leaders first convince themselves that they have the stuff of leaders. This is not as difficult as it sounds when you realize that most people need to follow, and will actually do better and be happier if they are led by a strong individual. People are not programmed robots. They are breathing, fearful beings who require and respect authoritative leadership. As a leader with personal command power, you exert authority and win respect by:

(1) *Acting with confidence*
(2) *Using your decision power*

When you act with confidence, you exude authority. People take for granted that you *have* the authority to lead and will react accordingly. But the secret is to *act* confidently no matter the circumstances. When you do, you will win respect regardless of the situation.

An authority is expected to make precise, clean decisions. To win respect, the authoritative leader must use his mind to make trigger-quick decisions. He must answer questions with one definitive answer.

President Truman did not respect aides who lacked confidence or failed to make sharp, clear-cut decisions. He had little patience with aides who answered questions by telling the president he could do one thing on the one hand, or another thing on the other hand. In his salty way, he expressed a decided preference for "one-handed" authorities. Of course, Mr. Truman had a right to expect his aides to use their decision power. Practice and preparation will equip you to exert authority with confidence and decisiveness. The respect will automatically follow.

• Set the example

Your helpers will be more productive if you set the example. When the leader sets the example, others follow. If you set an example of hard work, it will be easy to motivate people to work hard for you. Leadership that sets the example leads, and leadership that sets the example wins respect.

• Be informed

When you establish a program to lead people into doing what you want, gather all possible information on your project. When you are well informed, you eliminate the risks involved in half-hearted leadership because the knowledgeable leader deserves and wins respect.

Merle Zimmerman leads a talented sales force of real estate agents whose respect she wins by using all the information available to her, which she gets by attending seminars, board meetings, conventions, and studying regularly. She uses her information to guide and direct, to push and lead, because she knows every phase of her business and is a forceful and informed lady. She has earned respect by using informed leadership.

• Establish time frames

Leadership that drags is not leadership that wins respect. To get things done, you must set time limits. Here are some power tips on when and how to establish time frames that will win respect.

- When you issue an order, that is the time to set a date for it to be filled and complete.
- If you make a request, emphasize exactly *when* you expect compliance.
- At all times, sound and act as if you expect goals to be met on time and name that time.
- Explain the penalties and losses that tardiness will entail.
- Emphasize why your time goals are reasonable and necessary.
- As you set up schedules for those you motivate and use, explain the steps they must take to be done on time.

When you establish time frames as a leader with ample PCP, you can expect to win respect right on schedule—your schedule.

HOW SUE McDANIELS WON RESPECT AND GOT A RAISE IN THE BARGAIN

Sue McDaniels worked in the office of a busy consumer product manufacturer. Sue was secretary to the younger brother, who was the more intelligent and business-wise of the two partners. Nevertheless, the elder brother would impulsively barge into the younger brother's office and create an unpleasant scene at the slightest pretext. For example, if a shipment of raw materials was late, the younger partner was raked over the coals; if cash receivables were slow in coming in, little brother was tongue-lashed unmercifully. The language was rough and the air charged. After three such episodes, all in the presence of the new secretary, Sue stood in front of the abusive brother and said, "Mr. Mayse, your brother may have to tolerate your senseless behavior but I don't. Either you get out of this office or I do." The younger man quickly arose at this point and said, "Ed, she's right. Get out and don't come back until you can remember this is a business place." Ed Mayse stood stunned for a minute, apologized, then left. The next week, Sue had a $100 raise and a note of appreciation signed by both brothers. She had used her leadership qualities to stop an ugly scene and had cleared the air. The raise and the respect she won from both men was richly deserved. The reaction of both men to her spontaneous display of PCP fully showed that Sue McDaniel had won what was due those who unhesitatingly take the lead.

SECRET POWER TIPS TO WIN THE RESPECT OF YOUR ASSOCIATES

There is universal conviction of the need for respect in today's society. This need reaches into government, business, education, religion and all aspects of public and institutional life, but it is felt most keenly in the everyday affairs of individuals. The respect of your associates is what counts the most. These secret techniques and examples illustrate how you can win such respect for yourself.

● Insist on your personal dignity

One strong way to win respect is to insist on being treated with dignity. I do not mean being coddled, but rather, treated as a peer with the intelligence and capacity to hold your own. You won't have to advertise in big bold letters that you expect and insist on a modicum of dignity. Your attitude and your PCP should make that perfectly plain to your associates. However, abrupt and forceful action sometimes is in order, when and if your immediate associates forget their manners temporarily.

T. J. Kendall lost the attention of a group of his associates while he was addressing them after dinner. In a misguided and crude attempt to quell the chatter, he picked up a spoon and threw it into the glassware at the center of the table. Suddenly, somebody with one martini too many threw it back at Mr. Kendall. Soon the air was full of silverware and glasses. The meeting broke up amidst a shambles, and Mr. Kendall never finished his speech. Obviously, he had failed to command the needed dignity, and also, had failed dismally to win any respect at the function where he was supposed to be the featured speaker!

By contrast, William B. Brian, a powerful motivational speaker, handled a similar situation by rapping for attention, then saying, "Gentlemen, I was paid three thousand dollars to address you tonight. Unless you can show me enough courtesy to listen, I will take the money and leave now." Silence settled over the room, and for the rest of the evening, Mr. Brian was the center of attention.

Now, let's examine these two examples. Who insisted on respect from his associates of the day? Who lost control because he failed to exercise dignity and strength? Mr. Brian, of course, won the respect and attention of his associates, and like Mr. Brian, you can effectively insist on your personal dignity with power.

The ground rule in winning respect from your associates is this: never allow them to take undue advantage of their familiarity or close relationship with you. It is often easy for a day-to-day associate to assume that he can work on your friendship and sympathy to extract lop-sided concessions from you. Of course, you do not want to keep up a running dogfight with the people you see most often since you can ill afford constant strife and stress. But, you can afford even less to abandon PCP and reason, just because a close associate may imply that a friendly relationship is at stake. When an associate asks for an advantage based on nothing more than the incidental fact that you are thrown together often, do this: keep your dignity, smile, and say "no." You will win his respect and keep his friendship. Your closest associate knows when he is unfairly playing on your friendship, but it can be handled, as one strong-willed man shows us.

Bruce Renner, a buying agent for a large metal products manufacturer, was told by one of his suppliers that due to their long and friendly association, he (the supplier) was sure that Bruce would agree to an immediate 5% to 7% over-the-board price increase. Bruce responded with firm dignity by saying that he had indeed enjoyed the relationship with the supplier, and that it saddened him to realize he was going to be forced to give all that good business to one of his newer associates. Obviously, the price increases were not put into effect and Mr. Renner had gained renewed respect by refusing to be conned into surrendering to his associate, who wanted to flim-flam him with the old "since we are friends" routine.

Respect and personal dignity do go hand in hand. You can have both.

YOU HAVE A FORCEFUL BUILT-IN COMMAND SOURCE

Respected leaders come in all shapes and sizes. Some are aggressive and authoritative by nature, while some have to work at it. Regardless of the type of leadership, all who lead must constantly exercise power, keep up-to-date in their sphere of operation (so as not to neglect the intelligence factor inherent in leadership), and use people. As a leader, you have a forceful built-in command source that can win respect. Even if you have not yet utilized this power secret fully, it is still there, nonetheless. If the spark were not there, you would not be learning power secrets at this very moment.

Keep your mind on this thought: you have the same equipment that all leaders use and you have the same built-in command source that demands respect. You can use that source to guide, direct, enable and inspire others to help you get what you want. You are holding an encyclopedia of techniques and how-to secrets in your hands right now.

HOW TO USE YOUR BUILT-IN POWER
ON A DAILY BASIS

Power is wonderful in a crisis situation but it is even stronger and more enduring (and wins more respect) when you apply it on a daily basis. Life is a short trip: don't hoard your PCP for special occasions. Use it every day and enjoy extra respect daily.

On a daily basis, there is not as much stress as when you only use your PCP in a crisis. There is also this advantage; when you use your power on a daily basis, people are reminded every day that you are in charge, and the person in charge always wins respect from friend and foe.

Try these ideas about techniques and the proper use of power to win and hold respect every day.

● Have a daily plan

The constructive and judicious use of power requires planning which is as important on a daily basis as plotting strategies for special goals or projects. An erratic whirlwind has power, but all it really does is raise dust. Power without purpose and direction wins only minimal respect.

One effective way to plan the use of your built-in power is to take pen and paper and briefly outline tomorrow. Many strong performers divide the day into hours so they know ahead of time where they will be and where their personal power must be applied every hour. This simple technique doesn't take long and it does give direction to your concentrated efforts.

Planning may not guarantee that your day will flow as easily as warm syrup, but it insures that your power will generate respect on a day-to-day basis.

● Present the same face each day

It is easy to slide into an unguarded, relaxed attitude after winning a power struggle, but in order to be a strong, programmed operator, you must present the same face each day. You cannot be a determined, hard-driving figure one day, and a relaxed, indifferent power figure the next. Power demands consistent, qualified action every day if it is going to win you respect. This does not mean that you have to be in a fire-fight before the sun goes down every day. It does mean that the people you influence and direct will be keeping a daily eye on you. When you consistently use your PCP to lead, you will consistently earn and command respect.

YOU CAN WIN RESPECT WITH RESPECT

When you influence and use people to strengthen your own position, it does not categorize them as weaklings unworthy of your respect. Rather, it compliments your choice of other strong characters who have the intelligence to appreciate and profit from power and constructive ability. You must give them their due respect for having contributed to your own PCP. Weaklings can contribute nothing, including respect, to further your projects. On the other hand, as you move and guide power-conscious associates, you will gain a generous portion of extra power plus respect. This adds immeasurably to your own momentum.

You can respect power-helpers without indulging in one iota of mushy sentimentality. Simply give them business-like respect as they earn it. They will repay you tenfold.

ANOTHER POWER SECRET THAT WINS RESPECT: RESPECT YOURSELF

Respect from other effective people, like power, begins within you. If you do not have respect for yourself and your own power, how can you expect your helpers to respect you? Conversely, the more respect you have for yourself, the more respect you will enjoy from your power-influenced associates, as well as from casual acquaintances.

How do you develop this self-respect? John Nokes, who once had an office in my building, had some ideas on the subject. John was a successful, money-making executive with so much self-regard that it bordered on egotism. John's ideas worked for him and they will work for you.

(1) Be visionary: see yourself as a competent, able, productive, constructive winner, and let nothing alter that view. Then set some goals.

(2) Do not pre-judge whether you are worthy of respect from yourself or others. Instead, put your power to work on your own goals as solid proof that you deserve respect from all angles.

(3) Do not impose pre-set limitations on yourself, but rather, let your power take you as far as you want to go.

(4) Visualize the end results you seek and look at what you have already accomplished, then use this as a stepping-stone to move ahead and get the desired results. Nothing generates self-esteem faster than direct, purposeful action centered on an established goal.

(5) Ask yourself this: how much respect do you want to win? Decide today, write it down, and make a firm commitment.

If you put John Nokes' ideas to work for you, along with the other power secrets now churning inside your mind, it will be enough to get you all the self-respect you will ever need. It is also a solid basis for winning respect from all other quarters.

INSTANT POWER POINTERS

- Respect must be commanded.
- It is a law of human nature to respect forceful personalities.
- Leaders win respect, and leadership:
    (1) Exerts authority.
    (2) Sets examples.
    (3) Establishes time frames.
    (4) Wins respect, on schedule.

- The respect of associates is vital to your self-interest.
- Let your built-in command source win respect for you.
- Use your power secrets to win respect on a daily basis.
- You can win respect with respect.
- The more self-respect you have, the more respect you will win from others.

12

How to Use Your PCP to Say No

You have the self-obligation to say no, and the exclusive right to decide when you want to say it. Exercising this right adds power to your PCP. PCP is for more than just getting people to say yes to you: it is also for saying no to anyone when your interests are threatened.

The ability to say no is a power tool.

YOU ARE DAILY BOMBARDED
AND CONDITIONED TO SAY "YES"

Every time you turn on your TV set, you are conditioned to say yes by smart advertising men who make fortunes conditioning you to buy whatever their sponsor sells. You are also conditioned to say yes when you read an ad in your daily paper. You are subtly persuaded by every biased columnist you read. The radio gets in its licks too, and many of the people you see each day will also be sweet-talking or brow-beating you to say it.

Now that we have defined the problem, let's examine what happens if you cave in and say yes to all these blandishments. First of all, you will sacrifice your PCP, besides experiencing an erosion of self-confidence, a loss of direction, and personal frustration. Fortunately, there is no reason why this should ever happen to you. The examples which follow make this point.

IT IS HEALTHY TO SAY NO

PCP cannot tolerate a pretense of neutrality because indecisiveness is anathema to power. It demands a yes or no attitude and cannot work in the gray areas of irresolution and vacillation. Self-power demands clear-cut statements and action. It is healthy to say no when a negative response makes sense for you.

Think of it this way: if you never said no to anybody or anything, you would never get or do what you want, because you would be a puppet on the end of everybody else's string. This would be a sick situation.

A healthy way to look at saying no is to realize you are not responsible for other people's problems. If you feel that you should say no to a request or an outright order, just say no and end the matter. If you try to explain your reasons, or if your tone is wavering and apologetic, whoever is trying to get you to say yes will only stand there and twist your arm a little harder. Say no, and make it stick: that is the healthy way.

When Tim Workman, a recent hotel management school graduate, had his first job as a trainee with a major chain, he was exhausted and his social activities were nil. Mr. Farthing, Tim's supervisor, also called him regularly to substitute during other people's shifts in addition to his own. Finally, Tim decided to assert his right to say no, and it went as recorded below:

Mr. Farthing: "Tim, I want you to work Gregg's shift tonight. He won't be here."

Tim: "No, I'm not available tonight, Mr. Farthing."

Mr. Farthing: "What do you mean you're not available? Are you ill?"

Tim: "No. I'm just not available."

Mr. Farthing: "But I need you. You've always been available. Why aren't you available tonight? It wouldn't hurt you to work for Gregg, would it?"

Tim: "No. I'm just not available tonight, Mr. Farthing."

After a bit more of this broken-record routine on Tim's part, Mr. Farthing sighed and said he guessed he would just have to find someone else to work Gregg's shift. Tim didn't work that night, and Mr. Farthing stopped asking him to fill in for every absentee. Furthermore, he stopped thinking of Tim as a young kid who could not say no.

It is often healthy to say no. Now you have the prescription.

WHEN TO SAY NO

How do you know when someone is pushing you to acquiesce to his demands? How do you recognize it when someone has overstepped the bounds of assertive behavior? You will know it is time to say no when (1) you simply do not want to say yes, and (2) you get that uncomfortable, queasy feeling that someone is trying to get you to do something you do not want to do.

These instinctive feelings tell you when to say no. Any time you feel them is the time to unhesitatingly and unequivocally say no.

There are other times and situations when you should say no. For instance, when you are asked to do something that inconveniences you unnecessarily and, at the same time, provides an undeserved benefit to another party.

Example: "John, will you punch in for me? I'm running late."

This is a friend asking you to stick your neck out because he is not performing. This is a good time to say no.

Example: "Mary, since today is your day off, will you mind little Willie for me?"

Another "friend" is trying to con Mary into giving up her day off from a busy office job so that she, the friend, can do as she pleases. This sort of imposition can get to be a habit, and the answer is no.

Example: "Hey, Joe, loan me $200 until pay day. I bet on the wrong team last week!"

This one wants to use you as his interest-free banker so he won't be inconvenienced by his own foolish habit. This is the time to keep your money and say no.

Example: "Old Buddy, run over to Kumquat's today and sell him 100 widgets for me. That will make my quota for the month and I won't miss my bonus."

To heck with *your* quota. This guy wants you to fill *his* for him. The "no" should be really loud and clear here.

In all walks of life, you will find that there are people who will hit you with seemingly harmless requests that are actually treacherous. In every case, though he or she may not be willing to admit it, somebody is trying to maneuver you into being a fall guy. When you sense that you are being suckered into the role of a patsy, forget friendship. Being friends is great, but when you are being used for somebody else's convenience, that's the time to say no!

HOW TO SAY NO AND FEEL GOOD ABOUT IT

A difficulty strong personalities must often deal with when saying no is the gnawing, disturbing feeling that perhaps they have committed an offense. This is perfectly natural since self-power does not obliterate all sensitivity. Rather, the stronger and more effective one becomes, the more aware he is of other people's problems. However, no matter how strong you may become, you cannot drastically alter the personality and thought processes of others. You can, however, control their actions and thinking. This can often be accomplished by saying no. And you frequently do the other party a favor in the bargain. Here is an example:

Jim Rollins, sales manager for Whitlock Machinery and Manufacturing, Inc. was approached by Yates Trotman, their young accountant. The young man insisted that he be given a sales territory recently vacated by a retiree, but Jim Rollins said no because he knew the young man was introverted, disliked making decisions, and was uncomfortable around strangers. Trotman was angry and upset when Mr. Rollins said no, but six months later he came to Jim Rollins and thanked him for it. He explained that he had been talking with the company's salesmen and had learned enough to convince him that he wasn't cut out for sales work.

Jim feels good about saying no. He protected his own and

the company's interests. Yates is pleased too because he's now
the company's comptroller.

J. D. Elswick, senior partner of a prosperous brokerage
firm, was approached by Samuel Lockhart, another member of
the firm. Sam had a red-hot idea to put most of the firm's money
into a new, highly promoted farm cooperative. The dividends
were fantastic and the sales program couldn't fail according to
Sam, but J. D. Elswick said no. For six months the air was so
thick it could be sliced with a dull knife, until a scandal surfaced
and the co-op went under. The principals had been arrested and
charged with a multitude of high crimes. J. D. had saved his firm
with a convincing "no." Samuel Lockhart was among those
expressing genuine gratitude to J. D.

When you have the facts and your judgment tells you to say
no, the best way to do it is to come right out with it. You can
smile when you say no under these circumstances, since they
are smiles of iron and fire. Your opposition will understand,
sooner or later, that you did the right thing by saying no when
he was harassing you to say yes, and you can feel good about
that too.

SECRETS TO USE TO SAY NO
AND STILL KEEP YOUR FRIENDS

Nobody wants to lose a friend, yet if a friendship is so fragile
that an honest and forthright "no" might terminate it, then there
is hardly enough friendship involved to be concerned about. No
friend has the right to ask you to violate sound judgment or
abandon your PCP. In any event, you can say no to your friends
and still keep them. Try these secret techniques.

When a friend asks you to do something you can't,
shouldn't, or simply don't want to do, model your reply along
these lines:

"No, Jim, even though you are a dear friend."

"No, Clarke, and I expect you to understand."

"No, Mary, it's impossible."

"No, Dick, not even for you."

"No, and I'm sure you can appreciate my position."

"No, in fairness to both of us."

"No!"

You can soften the blow with some harmless qualifying statement when you are compelled to say no to a friend. This way you can keep your power intact while preserving your friendship. But in the end it is better to lose a weak, short-sighted friend rather than give up your PCP.

HOW TO SAY NO WITHOUT BEING NEGATIVE

When you say no for whatever reason, you are rejecting an idea or request that you cannot endorse. You are not necessarily rejecting the person presenting the idea or making the request. If your answer consists of only that one little power word "no," the tone of your voice, your expression, your gestures, and your total body language can round out your meaning fully. No is a matter-of-fact word. It need not be splintered and fragmented with personal animosity. Your "no" is based on your judgment and on the dictates of your power, not on pique or personalities. It is not a temperamental, negative action, but rather a positive power statement and should be handled as such.

Lois Cole is a supervisor in a garment factory which employs over a hundred women. She is obliged daily to say no, and she never hesitates to say it when she must. She looks the other person squarely in the eye, and with a slight wave of her right hand, says no in a tone that clearly means, "Now, you know I can't do that even though you're a good kid."

Lois gets no back talk because she says no emphatically, without being negative.

Keep your "no" clean and cool. Center it on the issue as Lois does. This way you will get a strong point across without being negative. "No" *is* a positive power statement.

HOW TO SAY NO TO THE PUSHY TYPE

You will encounter some persistent characters who can't seem to take no for an answer. These pushy types will try to keep the pot boiling in the belief that if they push hard and long enough, you will fold up. If you show any sign of weakening, look out! You are in for a long session of harassment.

The pushy type will probe and pry to keep the issue open by using such questions and pleas as:

(1) "But why?"

(2) "I just can't understand your thinking."

(3) "I'm absolutely bewildered by your answer."

(4) "What harm would it do if you agree to do it my way?"

(5) "What's the matter? Don't you trust me?"

(6) "How can you say no to a good friend?"

(7) "I hope you're joking!"

(8) "Where does that leave me?"

(9) "What will Mamie think when I tell her you flatly said no?"

(10) "Don't you ever consider the other person's feelings?"

(11) "That's cruel. You just have to reconsider."

(12) "You can't mean no!"

The list is endless; however, these examples are enough to give you the idea. Now, using the following rebuttals as models, you can silence your tormentors once and for all.

(1) "The answer is no. I see no reason to explain."

(2) "I'm sure you can't, but the answer is still no."

(3) "Don't be confused. I plainly said no."

(4) "Probably none, but my answer is no."

(5) "The answer is no. Trusting you has nothing to do with it."

(6) "It's strictly impersonal, but it is no."

(7) "The answer to that is also no."

(8) "Right where you were before I said No."

(9) "Mamie is not my problem."

(10) "Certainly. Mine also. No is final."

(11) "I've reconsidered. The answer is no."

(12) "I mean no."

Use these suggestions along with your own power ploys that you will develop with study and practice. Once you have said no, don't be brow-beaten into changing your position merely because somebody goes into a little act. The dramatics are just for effect. Don't be bamboozled. A legitimate "no" does not need to be propped up by a lengthy argument. In fact you should

KEEP IT SIMPLE

One of the cornerstones of PCP is the ability to say no when it serves your best interests to do so. The most effective—and the most painless—way to say no is simply and straightforwardly. When you respond with an uncomplicated "no," it has the ring of authority. The decision has been made, expressed, and the door to further discussion or bickering has been closed.

You can also use these other techniques when necessary.

• When you say no simply and forcefully, you give the opposing party credit for being able to understand the reasons for it. If he cannot understand your thinking, it will help neither of you to entangle yourselves in a web of explanations.

• Furthermore, you do not raise false hopes when you issue a straight and simple "no." This saves the frustration of profitless haggling and the air is cleared because everybody knows exactly where they stand. This is fair both to you and your opposition.

• You will develop a well-deserved reputation for having the power to handle pressure tactics when your "no" is as clean as an icicle. Only an indecisive personality says no with a question mark. When you say it simply and decisively, your reputation as a power figure is enhanced. This alone will spare you from having to say no many times, because those around you will learn that trivial, unreasonable requests will be shot down with that simple little word.

OTHER BENEFITS YOU WILL GAIN
FROM A SIMPLE "NO"

A simple "no" offers the strong, assertive individual a variety of benefits. The following list of those benefits will be enough to strengthen your determination to use your PCP to say no, simply and effectively.

When you are confronted with a negative demand and stop it with a plain "no," you will

- **Save time.**

A plain, simple "no" obviates the tug-of-war that a weak, plaintive "no" invites. "No" and a flat refusal to be led into an argument will save you time. It eliminates needless verbiage and the time-consuming, emotional strain that a weak "no" can precipitate. Say no, and save yourself a lot of wear and tear along with much precious time.

- **Save money.**

Where your money is at stake, a simple "no" will keep you out of trouble. There are well-planned strategies to trap the unwary into saying yes, thereby investing or giving their money to questionable enterprises. Those who are after your money anticipate a "no." They come prepared to attack your decision. A "no" that closes the case will save you money, too.

- **Puts you in the dominant position.**

A final "no" gives you the upper hand since the most belligerent, aggressive opponent is helpless when you say no and refuse to be dragged into further discussion. A simple, direct "no" is a strong statement which puts you in the dominant position.

- **Handles tough situations.**

When you face aggressive opposition or a persistent problem, the simple "no" is the best tool ever devised for handling it. The longer a bad situation or problem is drawn out, the tougher it becomes. But an outspoken, authoritative "no" will handle it and end the matter.

● **Keep your PCP growing.**

Each time you get on top with a simple "no," you add muscle to your PCP. When experience and skill prove the power of a simple "no," your confidence grows. With this added command power, you will never dread facing a confrontation that demands an outright "no." A forceful "no" will keep your PCP growing: it is a solid, one-word power technique.

HOW TO ANALYZE YOUR NEGATIVE RESPONSE

Your major yes or no decisions will not usually be thrust upon you like a bolt of lightning from out of the blue. In most cases, you will have time to analyze your negative response. However, do not agonize over it since this would only make your decision fuzzy and sap the vitality of your "no." The purpose of analyzing your response is to make it as strong and definitive as possible.

Try the following helpful exercise. Take a clean sheet of paper and draw a line down the middle. On one side, write "What I will gain by saying "no." On the other side write "Possible adverse effects." Now you are ready to write your strategy down in black and white, and then can see how the benefits will outweigh any possible losses. Your chart will be concrete, visible proof that your "no" is to your advantage. See the following example.

What I Will Gain with a No	Possible Adverse effects
Action	Ruffled feelings
Profit	Mock surprise
Money	Dramatics
Personal satisfaction	
Time	
Respect	
Prestige	
Authority	
Domination	
Power	
Friends	

An extra benefit you will gain from making this power chart to support your planned "no" response is the expertise and confidence that this practice gives you. It will equip you to say no when an unexpected attack or event is thrust upon you.

SECRET TECHNIQUES THAT
MAKE YOUR "NO" FINAL

There will be occasions when some obtuse, hostile party might find it difficult to accept your "no." Nevertheless, there are quick, effective techniques to deal with this problem. Build on the following concepts.

• You can say no and show the antagonistic party out the door. The next example explains how one business man used this technique.

Jack Bridges, president and owner of Bridges Fasteners, Inc., had just said no to a solicitor whose political cause he was opposed to. However, Walter Kahn, the red-faced and defiant solicitor, kept insisting. Jack Bridges rose, walked around his desk, held open the door and motioned Kahn outside. Kahn got the message. The no was final and he blustered out as Mr. Bridges calmly went back to work.

• You can say no and then pull the curtain on further time-wasting discussion by simply saying no and walking away. This technique has the ring of finality. When you say no, then turn your back and walk away to something else, your opponent knows it is all over. Use your walking shoes when you must: this will give weight and finality to your "no."

• Another gimmick that dismisses unwanted, annoying pressure is to say no and reach for the telephone. If your opponent insists on further appeals, keep on talking into the phone. He won't hang around long.

If a phone is not handy, start reading some reports or papers. Even the most thick-skinned adversary will quickly realize that your "no" is final because you've locked him out mentally.

• Hang the sign of finality on your "no" by implied ridicule: merely utter a disarming, "Now you know that I can't do that! No!"

The implication here is that it's obvious this person who is needling you for a yes is too smart to expect anything but a no. Your use of such oblique ridicule will make him aware that you see through his ruse, and he will soon be gone.

- Another useful device for making a "no" final is to look up when your visitor persists and say, "I don't think you heard me. I said no." Unless he is looking for a fight, your unwelcome guest will leave. If he doesn't, add on the other technique of showing him the door as in our first example.

- You can also say no and add the polite phrase, "Excuse me. I have work to do." Or, "Aunt Agnes is waiting," or whatever. As we just noted, you can use more than one technique to make your "no" final. Just don't make a federal case of it: the brief, matter-of-fact no is no, and final is final.

The purpose of a "no" is not to brutalize, embarrass, or start fights. Rather the purpose of a strong "no" is to protect and preserve your interests—your PCP. There is no reason for you to feel squeamish about saying it in the most effective manner that you possibly can. It is self-preservation. It is an absolute necessity in today's rivalry and competition. It is a little word with a lot of wallop.

INSTANT POWER POINTERS

- You have the right to say no.
- You are conditioned to say yes.
- It is healthy to say no.
- There is a time to say no.
- You can say no and feel good about it.
- You can say no and still keep your friends.
- Center your "no" on the issue.
- "No" is a positive power statement.
- Don't be bamboozled by the pushy types.
- Keep your "no" simple.
- Chart your negative response for greatest impact.
- Make your "no" final.
- No is no. Final is final.

13

Getting Rid of Fear

Everybody is afraid of something. This is a perfectly normal, healthy protective instinct as old as time itself. Our concern here is with abnormal fears that erode power, self-confidence, and sound reasoning.

This chapter does not propose to deal with a national or world-wide malaise. Rather, it is designed to put your personal fears in perspective and give you the secrets to overcoming fears that might threaten or weaken your personal command power.

Man's capacity for self-delusion is unlimited, and many of his personal fears are without basis, often bordering on the irrational. Such fears can hide PCP behind a cloud of the darkest confusion. However, this need not be your problem.

HOW TO USE PERSONAL COMMAND POWER
TO OVERCOME FEAR OF FAILURE

One of today's more common fears is that of failure. Our society is so success oriented that failure is tantamount to disgrace in the minds of many victims of fear. Success means approval and acceptance; to fail means to suffer shame. Success spells superiority. Anything less is regarded as inferiority. Thus goes the reasoning of those who fear failure.

What is this terrible fear of failure? One definition applies to all forms of fear: it is an unpleasant, often strong emotion caused by anticipation of danger or impending disaster. The key word in this definition is *anticipation*. We anticipate disaster even where there is no cause for such dread. In fact, much fear has no logical basis. However, this does not lessen its debilitating effect upon those who are afflicted with the painful fear of failure.

How can one deal with this power-robbing emotional state, this fear of failure? The following secrets of PCP cover effective methods for controlling this gnawing malady. Put them to work today if you are being victimized by the self-torturing fear of failure.

● Recognize that success is relative

That which spells success for one man may hold no interest for another. For example, the man striving to become an electronics engineer could care less about trucks and trucking. On the other hand, a husky young truck driver's idea of the ultimate success could be to own his own rig. Success is relative to what *you* want. Don't make the mistake of trying to be the success somebody else may envision for you. Success founded on anything less than your own personal goals will certainly be less than gratifying. If you attain success in what you choose to do or become, that is enough. This concrete view of the elements of success should wipe out any of your fears of failure.

● Set realistic goals for yourself

It is self-punishment to work toward goals you are not suited to either by temperament or training. Attaining your goal is success. Personal success, like personal power, can leap-frog from one goal to a higher goal. Check your qualifications. Establish as tough a goal as you can reasonably hope to attain. This will block out your fears of failure and keep you on the road to success as the next example illustrates.

Cliff Lomax was fresh out of college and his idea of success was to become president of a national concern. Cliff was a realist who knew that his success would come in steps. His first

move was to apply for a position in the accounting department
of the giant company he had selected. When he succeeded in
landing this job, he set his eyes on the comptroller's spot. From
this goal, he reached for and attained the presidency: the final
goal in his campaign for success.

Note that Mr. Lomax didn't start with a goal he was not yet
equipped to handle. Instead, he dismissed all fear of failure by
setting one realistic goal, then preparing for the next. This workable, rewarding technique eliminates any reason to fear failure.
It is a proven power technique.

- ## Don't regard a set-back as failure

There is no need to think of every small defeat as a total
failure. A set-back should be a temporary event; a time for
learning and regrouping. Few, if any, major successes are
gained without some set-backs. Any successful man will tell you
that, yes, he had his nose bloodied a few times along the way,
but that this did not cause him to give in to the fear of failure.

Focus your PCP on these three keys which will put your
fears of failure into proper perspective. You can then go on to as
much success as you can stand.

(1) Recognize that success is relative.
(2) Set realistic goals for yourself.
(3) Don't regard a set-back as a failure.

These three are enough to turn your power loose.

SECRETS TO WHIPPING THE FEAR
OF "THE BIGGIES"

One of the most demeaning of all fears is that of those
people who have, or seem to have greater power, prestige,
wealth or position than you. This fear of "The Biggies" is not
justified, because no matter how high a man or woman rises, he
or she is still burdened with mortality and the limitations that it
imposes upon each of us. True, men who reach the top have
exercised a lot of power along the way, but this does not mean
they will gobble you up at first sight.

Use these positive techniques to whip any fear of the big-gies.

(1) In dealing with a fear of "The Biggies," keep in mind that the higher a man rises, the quicker he will recognize and respect power in his contemporaries. By definition you must decide how much power you have, because it lies there within you. In order to be appreciated, your power must be put into action to be seen and understood. To whip the fear of "The Biggies," you must do the following things.

You must admit that you fear failing to perform successfully in the presence of Mr. Big. Now analyze that emotion, and ask yourself if it is warranted. As soon as you realize that you are only afraid of something that might happen, not something that is destined to happen, you will be in a strong position to elim-inate your fear. The secret is to speak and act as if you feel powerful and confident. This takes thought, determination, and practice. All the rehearsal will pay off. When you act and speak as if power and confidence are surging through you, Mr. Big will accept you as his equal, which, indeed, you are!

Janet Piper, a newspaperwoman, had been handed the assignment of interviewing Mr. B. Arch Dobbs, a tough, irasci-ble, and highly successful business man. Everybody, including Janet, quaked at the thought of facing this brusque character. Janet decided that the only way to get anything from this indi-vidual was to meet him on his own level. So she brashly ignored his secretary, walked to his desk, and stated that she was a newspaper reporter there to get a story from him. She sat down and suggested that they get started since his time was valu-able, and she had a deadline to meet. The old boy was briefly stunned, but he then guffawed and said, "Young lady, I like your style."

Of course, Janet conducted an excellent interview because she had done a masterful job of dealing with her fear of "The Biggies." She got what she was after, along with admiration and cooperation from the man she was supposed to fear. When you use your PCP to deal with "The Biggies" as Janet did, your power will be recognized and your fears will dissipate like dew in the morning sun. Fear-challenging behavior is a sure sign of inner power. When you practice such conduct regularly, your

fear of the biggies will melt away along with any other ground-
less fears that may be haunting you.

HOW TO KILL THE FEAR OF RISK-TAKING

In a security-conscious society that mistakenly believes
every step in life should be protected, shielded, and guaranteed,
being afraid of risk-taking is understandable. It is also crippling
and frustrating. Nothing is gained without risk. You cannot
cross the street without risking your life, you can't get out of bed
without risking a broken leg. Since risk-taking is a fact of life,
where is the logic in fearing it?

This is not to suggest that you should ignore the element of
risk and rush pell-mell into every situation that might flash
across the screen. Risk cannot be eliminated. It can, however, be
curtailed and minimized with some prudence and thought.
Before becoming afraid, try the following steps:

(1) Evaluate your chances.
(2) Go ahead if the odds favor your success.
(3) Plan the outcome before you take action.
(4) Be prepared to face a loss.
(5) Don't risk more than you can afford to lose.
(6) Work as if you never expect to lose.

You can eliminate the fear of risk by going into things with
your eyes open. Gauge your risks along these six steps, each of
which are applicable to any form of risk, whether concrete
business ventures or something designed only to draw attention
to yourself or your work. Now let's see how one man lost his fear
of risk-taking.

HOW NED POWERS WENT OUT ON A
LIMB AND LOST HIS FEAR

Ned Powers was a forty-one-year-old father of two, and a
successful salesman for an automotive parts firm. Although Ned

felt sure he could do even better as an independent representative in the business, he was well aware of the risks involved. A nagging fear of taking the risk held him back for several years. He keenly felt his responsibility to his family. At the same time he was convinced that he owed it to both his family and himself to do the best he could for them. Finally Ned took stock. He had twenty years of road experience in the business, good health, an excellent following of dealers, enough cash to finance himself for a full year, and a determination to win. This was enough to remove all fears of risk. He promptly mailed the following letter to three automotive parts suppliers.

> Gentlemen:
>
> The first of the year I am going out on my own as an independent sales representative, and you are important to my plans.
> I have twenty years of experience selling automotive parts. I also have a large and loyal dealer following in the territory, plus the expertise and financial reserves to insure my success as an independent agent.
> I am acquainted with your firm and your product line, and I feel certain that an association with you will prove mutually profitable.
> If you wish, I will be more than pleased to furnish any other information you require.
> May I hear from you? It is not too early to plan for a big year together.
>
> Sincerely,
>
> Ned Powers

Within three weeks, Ned had an agreement with the two largest suppliers. He picked up an additional line only one month after launching his new career. His risk-taking (or rather his getting rid of his fear of risk) has doubled both his income and his job satisfaction.

True, Ned went out on a limb, but not blindfolded. Here's how he handled the fear of risk.

• He evaluated his chances and saw that they were good since he had been making it for twenty years as a company rep.

• He went ahead because the odds were in his favor since he had an excellent following.

• He planned well: he had saved the money for the new venture, and had pre-selected the principals he wished to represent.

• He was prepared to face loss because his savings would protect him from total disaster.

• He was not risking more than he could afford.

• He worked as if he expected to win.

You can kill any fear of risk-taking just as Ned did, by analyzing your situation. If the odds favor you, jump in. If not, restructure your thinking and your resources, then proceed. The winners will all tell you that the risks are actually half the fun.

HOW TO END THE FEAR OF FINANCIAL FAILURE

In today's world, money is the most common yardstick used to measure personal worth. We won't debate the pros and cons of this system. It is enough to recognize and deal with it. It is not enough, however, to say that money ends the fear of financial failure. It is a matter of how much money. What is enough for one man, may leave another quaking in his boots. We cannot all be millionaires. Most of us could live with less than we have, although I abhor the thought of any man not doing or being the best he can—financially or otherwise. But I hold that the fear of financial failure should not be a chilling, lifetime experience. Use this reality to end the fear of financial failure: money that is lost can be regained; fortunes that are destroyed can be rebuilt. It is the *fear* of financial failure that is deadly.

Matt Goodrich had such a consuming fear of financial failure, that he refused to spend a dime that he did not have to give up for essentials. Consequently, his life was drab and barren, until one day it dawned on him, after a lengthy discussion with a friend, that he would not live forever. Suddenly, he bought a new house, a new car, and a new wardrobe for his wife. The atmosphere brightened. Matt took a renewed interest in life. Instead of hoarding his money, he began investing it. To his surprise, his money-making ability grew. He worked with renewed energy and found much satisfaction in putting his money into circulation. Now he no longer fears financial failure. He says it's because he is too busy enjoying his money to worry about it.

As Matt learned, fear of financial failure is an attitude which can be changed. If fear of financial failure torments you, reread this section and use Matt Goodrich's secret to rid yourself of this debilitating phobia.

HOW TO MAKE A POSITIVE RESPONSE TO FEAR

Dealing positively with fear will rid you of it. To maintain a direct, simple, workable method of dealing with fear, use this list of everyday worries and their positive responses which can erase the menacing scarecrow of fear from your thinking and your life.

Item: Fear of rejection

Response: It is the norm to want to be accepted by one's peers but it is self-destructive to fear nonacceptance. The positive thing to do is to conduct yourself as you feel is appropriate, then let the chips fall where they may. You can never expect to win the admiration of everyone, but when you conduct yourself with PCP that bespeaks your interests and abilities, you will be accepted by more than your share of interesting and successful people. This will keep you busy and productive, and it will also push out any nagging fears of social rejection.

Item: Fear of criticism

Response: This is a common fear of those who have not yet mastered the technique of PCP. At this point it should be of no concern to you. However, by way of review, the positive response to this ungrounded fear is to remember that it is nothing more than an opinion. It is not gilt-edged, irreversible, or fact. It may be sincerely delivered, but this does not guarantee that it is either deserved or true. So, take criticism for what it is: somebody else's opinion. If you can profit from it, fine; if not, reject it. By all means, refuse to fear it because it is a bugaboo, and PCP can make short work of a bugaboo.

Item: Fear of making a mistake

Response: People with PCP do things, and people who do things make mistakes. The only individuals who never make mistakes are those who do nothing. As a power figure, you are going to be involved in many activities, so an occasional mistake is inevitable. Profit by it, correct it, and move on. Remember, the fear of making a mistake is a paralyzing ghost; when you recognize that it has no substance, that it is a fear of the inevitable, you can get a handle on it. Then, concentrate on putting your power into doing what you want to do and getting what you want. You will see that the ratio of successes to failures will be favorable, so put this fear to rest.

Item: Fear of change

Response: Change is certain, and businesses, institutions, societies, individuals, and nations all change. The positive power approach to change is to study it, anticipate it, roll with the punches and profit by it. Your PCP is a viable force in the midst of change. This, along with observation and a keen interest in what is going on around you will obliterate any fears of change.

Item: Fear of verbal abuse

Response: Facing what you fear is called courage, but it could well be called personal command power. You can face up to verbal abuse and overpower your abuser with whatever means you choose, or you can walk away. Realize that verbal abuse is the way of weakness, so face up to it in your own style and dispose of it with your own PCP.

Item: Fear of losing

Response: If you are afraid of losing, ask yourself this: "What is the worst that would happen if I lose?" This question will cut the fear of losing down as it reveals that the loss can be handled. Your PCP is for winning: this is the attitude that puts the fear of losing away.

Item: Fear of exposing ignorance

Response: Will Rogers had the proper answer to this one. Will said, in effect, "Everybody is ignorant, except on different things." If you feel the need for more information on any subject, it is available to you from libraries, friends, teachers, executives, and experts in every field. Your determination, coupled with your personal power, can make you knowledgeable in any field.

Here is another positive idea to use in responding to fear:

● Any time you feel yourself being victimized by fear, ask yourself what you are gaining from it. Then, ask yourself what you would gain by dismissing your fears. The answers may change your life. The following case will clarify my point.

Foster Rigby, division manager for a national firm, had received a curt note from a Mr. James Blackwood, the brash new supervisor for the area. Mr. Rigby was advised that he was being summarily transferred to a less desirable division. Realizing that he had nothing to gain by hesitant fear and everything to gain by acting from strength, Rigby went to see Mr. Blackwood, who was formally introduced to him as *Mr.* Blackwood by the secretary. "Jim," said Rigby, "I'm here to tell you I can't accept that transfer."

Foster Rigby won because he had gained the instant advantage by calling the high-handed supervisor "Jim." This indicated his fear had been discarded and that his power was working—which it was, and perfectly!

TEST YOURSELF TO CHASE FEAR

You can't get rid of any kind of fear unless you test yourself by putting your PCP into action. If you are victimized by the fears we have detailed in this section, or any of the pernicious fears that can crowd reason from the mind, the key is to take advantage of the power techniques, the experience, and the ideas made available here. This will lead to personal action, which is the test that chases fear.

CHECKLIST

This checklist will help you keep fear under control, and can also be used as a self-test to determine whether you are operating with personal command power. Ask yourself the following questions.

1. Do you ask for a raise when you know you deserve one?
2. Do you habitually defer to others?
3. Do you refuse to do menial jobs that you detest?
4. Do you refuse to take meaningless orders?
5. Do you accept mistakes as the price of action?
6. Do you brush petty criticism aside?
7. Are you willing to take a risk to get what you want?
8. Do you act like a winner?
9. Do you place "The Biggies" above yourself?
10. Are you willing to risk your money for possible gain?

If you answer yes to all except numbers 2 and 9, you are operating with power. If not, you can analyze your position and use your command power to rid yourself of any fears that still plague you. This is a short list, but it is enough for a basis with which to construct your own checklist. When you mentally test yourself, you are taking a power step. Remember, being candid takes power, and your PCP can truly rid you of any fear when you put it into action.

INSTANT POWER POINTERS

- Man's capacity for self-delusion is unlimited.
- Fear of failure makes you your own victim.
- Fear of "The Biggies" is demeaning.

- Risk-taking can be half the fun.
- Financial failure is not terminal, rather it is the fear of financial failure that kills.
- A positive response gets rid of fear.
- You gain nothing from fear.
- Test your command power to chase fear.
- A self-test helps you operate with personal command power.
- Personal command power can rid you of any fear.

14

How to Pack Your Speech with Power

Speech is strong stuff: words, delivered with the personal command power of compelling speakers, have won more wars than mighty armies, and fiery, strong words have changed the course of societies. The masterful use of speech has exploded and expanded the personal power of leaders and winners in every walk of life. It can do as much for you.

PERSONAL EXPRESSION IS THE FIRE OF COMMAND POWER

To emphasize the importance of putting power into your speech consider this: regardless of what other resources you may possess, it is virtually impossible to put your power to work unless you can speak effectively and forcefully. In order to direct, motivate, use, and influence others, you must be able to speak plainly and clearly. Otherwise, your instructions and orders would be misunderstood. In itself, poor speech indicates a lack of direction and power.

Now, this does not mean that every utterance must be prim, full of fancy words, and expressed with the exactness of an English professor. Rather, it means that your speech should be simple, plain, and to the point. Big words and flowery speech do not constitute power speech; however, working words, short, strong sentences, and firm, clear delivery will convey your ideas with clarity and force.

Since clear personal expression (the ability to speak with convincing authority) is the fire of command power, here are some simple secrets that can give extra firepower to your voice and speech.

● Words need help

No matter how well chosen, the words you use to influence and control people need extra help. The strongest words delivered with arrogance or strain will be self-defeating. According to speech experts, some otherwise strong individuals turn people off every time they open their mouths. The reason they put people off is not because of the words they use, but rather by the quality and tone of their voices. To compound this problem, your posture and facial expression, along with the attitude they reflect, can deaden the impact of what you say. But, this does not call for despair. You can utilize the following ideas to remedy any habits that may be hampering your verbal power.

How can you tell if your voice rankles, sounds unpleasant, is weak, or lacks authority? For a simple test, put your nose gently against the middle of this book and speak in your usual tone. What you hear is just about the way you sound to others. A better test is to turn on a tape recorder and forget it's there. Then, ask someone to do something, give an order, or issue a set of instructions. You may be surprised at what you hear.

However you test yourself, listen carefully. Some particular faults to identify are:

1. A monotonous tone.
2. Vocal strain.
3. High pitch or squeakiness.
4. Mumbling.
5. Too low or too soft a sound.
6. Hoarseness.

7. Slurring of words.

8. Too many "uhs" and "ahs."

9. Excessively slow speech.

10. Extremely fast speech.

11. Indifference.

12. Lack of intensity.

Any of these speech faults are power-robbers, but all of them are subject to correction. A brief analysis of each of these traits will show you how to overcome any that may be infringing on your command power.

1. A monotonous tone

A droning, monotonous tone will not stir anyone to do anything for you. To hold attention and make people perform for you, your voice must have hills and valleys of volume. The louder peaks emphasize the main points and call for positive, decisive action, while the quieter valleys soothe and reassure without relinquishing control. A change of pace creates excitement and expectation. Your voice commands attention, interest, and cooperation, while a monotonous tone is devoid of excitement and fervor and has little to recommend it. You will pack power into your speech when you put hills and valleys of excitement, enthusiasm, and leadership into your voice. This will keep your PCP on a high plane.

2. Vocal strain

Vocal strain is usually the result of nervous tension, but if you attempt to speak in a higher, or unnatural tone, your voice will also be strained. To avoid this problem, breathe deeply, slow down, relax a bit, and speak in your normal voice.

3. High pitch or squeakiness

This condition is usually brought about by strain, and will respond to the same treatment. Practice speaking on a solid, easily-heard level. Most speech problems will respond with this power-building exercise.

4. Mumbling

Mumbling is easy to correct, since all it requires is a conscious effort to speak clearly and with enough volume to be heard. If this doesn't work, a professional speech therapist is recommended.

5. Too low or too soft a sound

Whatever the cause, this habit is too costly for the power-minded because it is easily misread as a sign of meekness or indecision. More volume through controlled breathing and practice should end this fault.

6. Hoarseness

If your voice is hoarse and raspy, you will be difficult to understand. This unpleasant condition makes it hard to speak with variety and force. This condition can often be relieved temporarily by gargling with as warm a salt-water solution as you can stand. Drinking a cup of hot water can also help, and there are gargles available from drug stores. A conscious effort to speak clearly may be all that is needed, but in any case, if hoarseness is a chronic condition, see your doctor. The sooner you stop croaking, the sooner you can add power to your voice. It is worth the remedy.

7. Slurring of words

Unless there is a physical impediment, slurring is sheer carelessness. A bit of conscientious effort will eliminate this speech weakness, and once accomplished, you will see an immediate improvement in the effect your speech has on others.

8. Too many "uhs" and "ahs"

This is simply a bad habit. When you become aware of this annoying tendency to clutter your speech with meaningless sounds and pauses, you can set to work to knock it out. A little thought and practice will do it.

9. Excessively slow speech

Some individuals labor under the illusion that slow speech gives the impression of deep thinking and great intellectual expression. Not so. Slow speech bores people, loses their attention, and raises serious questions as to why the speaker is so handicapped. The remedy for this disturbing problem is simply to speed it up. When you do so, your power will gain momentum right along with your improved speech.

10. Extremely fast speech

Speech that comes at you with the staccato bark of a machine gun is exhausting to listen to because it puts the listener under an unrelenting strain. Instead of being totally attentive and responsive, he will merely hope that you will run through quickly. The prescription here is simple: be honest with yourself if you are spouting out words too quickly, and slow it down. Words that are run together lose their punch; so space them, spice them, and deliver them with deliberate force.

11. Indifference

If the speaker is indifferent about how he speaks or what he says, whoever he addresses will be even more indifferent. If the speaker is indifferent to how effectively he speaks, he is bound to have even less interest in PCP. Obviously, this does not apply to you, so your only concern in this department would be never to lapse into indifference, even in a careless moment.

12. Lack of intensity

Intensity is a quality frequently omitted from speech analysis, yet it is an electrifying, motivating element that packs extra power into every word. Intensity is described as an extreme degree of strength, force, or energy. It is the speaker's total concentration and conviction being relayed to the audience, whether that audience is one or many people. You have heard orators who have spoken with intense feeling; you have felt the power. So put intensity into what *you* say: it will add zip and lightning to your words. When you give orders or seek to convince someone with intensity in your voice and manner, you will get instant, positive results. Put intensity into your speech when you know your subject. Know what you want, believe in it, and practice your delivery. An impressive example of intensity is the blowtorch which focuses its force and energy on the work at hand, to the exclusion of all else. When you put this kind of force into your speech, you will compel instant, respectful attention.

SPEECH MECHANICS

The mechanics of speech are an integral element in packing power into your speech. As we have noted, powerful speech is more than the meticulous recitation of words. It involves the total individual: breath, muscles, gestures, facial expressions, and attitude. At this point, we will deal briefly with the physical mechanics of speech power.

Breath supports your words; your larynx controls the pitch; and your mouth shapes the words. If you run out of breath, you also run out of speech.

An excellent way to begin your voice control exercise is to stand or sit erect and practice exhaling. Big puffs are not important, and since words and volume are determined by your breathing, practice long, deliberate exhaling and count as you exhale. With practice, you will soon double the amount of words your breath will carry. Of course, there will be times when you will want to explode all the force and breath you have into one word: do so, because you can gulp a new supply into the bottom of your lungs in a flash and never miss a syllable. Practice breathing, posture, gestures, and a variety of pitches and styles. When you put all this excitement, intensity, and power into your speech nobody's eyes are going to glaze before you.

USE SHORT, SIMPLE SENTENCES
FOR EXTRA POWER

Not every sentence can or needs to be chopped off with four or five words. Such a sing-song effect sounds too monotonous to command attention, so use sentences that are long enough and powerful enough to express your ideas clearly, and vary the length of your sentences just as you must vary the tone, volume, and pitch of your voice for maximum impact. The key is to avoid long, ponderous sentences that obscure your meaning because the people you seek to influence will only move when your ideas and instructions are clearly defined and easily understood. Short sentences, packed with powerful, simple words will do the job, as the following example shows.

A certain plumber had discovered that hydrochloric acid would do an excellent job of cleaning drains. But to be on the safe side, he wrote the appropriate bureau in Washington to find out if it was harmful.

Washington, with all deliberate speed, replied: "The efficacy of hydrochloric acid is indisputable, but the chlorine residue is incompatible with metallic permanence."

The plumber wrote back that he was happy the bureau agreed with him, at which time the bureau replied, more promptly, with a slight note of alarm: "We cannot assume responsibility for the production of toxic and noxious residues with hydrochloric acid and suggest you use alternate procedures."

The plumber, confused and befuddled, again replied that he was indeed happy that the bureau still agreed with him, "And well, thanks again."

This time Washington shot back this reply, "Don't use hydrochloric acid. It eats the hell out of pipes."

I leave it to you. Which reply moved the plumber to do what he should have done?

BUSINESS DEMANDS POWER SPEECH

Power speech, which is the same thing as effective speech, is so important in the complex business world of today that many corporate giants send their executives and trainees to professional speech clinics. Much business is still conducted through meetings, so obviously the need for effective speech is paramount in this setting. Years ago, when business could be conducted on a more intimate, personal basis with eyeball to eyeball contact, neither strong impressive speech nor good writing was always an absolute. But that is no longer the case.

Because we need to develop articulate speech in order to make it in the business world, we often hear the complaint that high school graduates can't speak effectively. The problem drives home the fact that power speech is essential to your business success, which you can insure by studying and practicing the power points made in this chapter. They are valid, workable, and they are for you, because they will enforce your PCP in business, informal, and public speech.

HOW I LICKED THE FEAR OF PUBLIC SPEAKING

I must make one point right at the beginning of this personal example: self-confidence is the one biggest secret in building PCP. Public speaking and the ability to speak to and control groups, is the quickest, most dynamic, and most gratifying shortcut to self-confidence. I know: I tried it. It works!

When I was a young junior executive, I was plagued by apprehension and uneasiness when obliged to speak before a group. Recognizing that the emotional strain it caused was unjustified and destructive, I determined to overcome this self-imposed handicap, and set about to become a dynamic, enthusiastic public speaker, no matter how large or small the audience. It was one of the most rewarding decisions of my life.

First, I attended a college speech class, three evenings a week, for a semester. Next, I bought a textbook and studied some basic principles: physical behavior on the platform, developing vocal variety, speech preparation, making an outline, parliamentary law, etc. But I still did not learn to speak because during the whole course, each student only made one three-minute speech! You can never learn public speaking without making speeches, and one three-minute speech certainly will not do it.

After completing that course, I decided to join a speech club, and selected what had to be one of the finest speech clubs in the land: the Senate Speakers' Club, which met regularly at the Dallas YMCA. As its critic, the club had S. Austin Weir, the renowned attorney and speech expert extraordinaire, who was also a superb instructor. Each member made a speech of his own choice at every meeting, then Mr. Weir criticized both the speech and the speaker's performance. He gave praise where praise was due, but he could also take the hide off a speaker who did less than his best. He also gave help where help was deserved. He was an exacting taskmaster, a friend, and an inspiring human being who presided over this club full of doctors, lawyers, preachers, executives, teachers, and sales people. His contribution to each of us was enormous, because he made us speak, speak, and speak. I am deeply indebted to this man and to the Senate Speakers' Club of Dallas which honored me by electing me its president during my second year of membership.

The point of this personal story is this: to learn to speak in public, you *must* speak in public. Take a course in public speaking, join a speech club, and then make speeches. Church groups and civic and service organizations all actively seek strong speakers, so take advantage of every opportunity to speak. Soon you will lick any fear of public speaking just as I did. You will be in demand, and your self-confidence will soar as you pack more and more power into your speech.

POWER SECRETS THAT CONTROL AUDIENCES

There are almost as many secrets to controlling audiences as there are speakers. Speaking is a personal, individual undertaking; your style is yours and no one can take it away from you. But there are three power techniques common to all power-loaded speakers, each of which will help you too.

(1) enthusiasm
(2) urgency
(3) intensity

Enthusiasm reflects your own interest in what you are saying, so it is important to understand the different applications of it. A common misconception about enthusiasm is that it always causes an excited, bouncy, bubbling performance. Enthusiasm, to engage power, must have more substance than this. In fact, a speech based on nothing more than an exhibition of enthusiasm and personal opinion will get you little besides the exercise. Yet enthusiasm can be, and often is, a component of urgency and intensity that conveys earnestness, conviction, and action. It says, "I believe this, follow me."

Inject enthusiasm into your power speech, but recognize it for what it is: an extra spark of personality used to add fire and conviction to what you say.

A speech that does not call for action is purely entertainment. There is nothing wrong with this if entertainment is the purpose of your speech, and there are speakers who specialize in it. However, we are dealing with stronger medicine, so our concern is packing power into what you say. Urgency lends itself to power: it calls for action now. To observe this, watch the fiery TV evangelists who forcefully urge the sinner to repent *now* and appeal urgently for funds, *now*. Their skillful use of urgency as a power technique in their speech is proven by their success. You can profit by their example. Put urgency into your speech to add power that controls and moves audiences to work for you.

Intensity shows burning conviction and urgency is evident in the voice and face of the speaker. To see what I mean, watch politicians speak: their intense manner cries out that the world is on fire and only they can save it.

Practice until you feel just such intensity in your speech and delivery, and remember that intensity packs power.

The last, vital secret is that if you do not control an audience, then nothing else counts. As your skills grow with practice, you will automatically develop your own techniques for controlling your audiences. But in the meantime, there are books devoted to this and other speaker's problems and you can take advantage of the authors' experience. Study their power techniques, and add them to your own. The next example was gleaned from one powerful speaker's control techniques and will give you something to build on.

A number of years ago, a prominent, high-priced speaker was being introduced by the mayor of a large city, who quipped that the guest speaker was like an automatic vending machine: put in a dinner and up came a speech.

The speaker rose to polite applause, then commented that there was one difference between the mayor and himself: when the mayor put in a speech, up came your dinner!

The reaction was exactly what you'd envision. The speaker won and kept instant control, and the mayor kept quiet.

HOW TO CHOOSE POWER WORDS

Almost any audience will applaud glittering, meaningless generalities, because such speech makes no demands, raises no questions, and embraces no power. Speeches full of generalities and lacking power words may leave your listeners feeling comfortable, but will not move them to do anything for you.

In choosing everyday words as well as in public speech, select only those words that pack power, and that will motivate people for you. The following list contains a few of the simple, classic words used regularly by advertising men and sales people.

results	safe	guarantee
fast	amazing	save
tried	true	proven
established	respect	high
proud	honest	researched
tested	reliable	position
leader	powerful	winner
important	easy	money
go	watch	now

Although Chuck Geromo had many of the attributes of PCP, such as a striking physique, enthusiasm, urgency, and intensity, he was somehow failing as a salesman. Fortunately, a wise and experienced sales executive turned Chuck around by making him see that he was using words like confetti in the wind. In his eagerness, Chuck was literally talking his prospects out of doing anything for him by using an excited mixture of words. But with a bit of expert coaching, Chuck was soon using power words, and this, along with his own determination, is helping him make the most of a select group of power words. He calls it his "economics of power"; he is now in line for a transfer and rewarding promotion.

Using power words, keeping in control, and calling for

action will pack your speech with power. This is another golden key to getting whatever you want.

This reminds me of Mark Twain's dictum: "The difference between the right word and almost the right word is the difference between lightning and a lightning bug."

INSTANT POWER POINTERS

- Speech is strong stuff.
- Words need your help.
- Focus your speech like a blowtorch.
- Speech mechanics are a power element.
- Use short, simple sentences for extra punch.
- Business demands power speech.
- Public speaking builds self-confidence.
- Self-confidence is the cornerstone of power.
- You can lick the fear of public speaking.
- Three keys to audience control:

> enthusiasm
> urgency
> intensity

- Avoid generalities.
- Use words that pack power.

15

Power Psychology
That Wins Agreement
and Cooperation

Psychology is a "science" that lends itself to a variety of definitions of interpretations, some of which follow.

- Psychology is the science of human and animal behavior.
- Psychology is the study of the mind's life.
- Psychology studies the behavior of organisms.
- Psychology studies what makes people tick.
- Psychology studies what makes people act or react.
- Psychology deals with techniques that motivate and/or control people.
- Psychology is the study of the subconscious attitudes and values that drive you.

Do not let these multi-faceted definitions of psychology mislead or discourage you. Psychology is real and people's minds are influenced by what comes into them. People are also influenced by the psychological impact of strong personalities, which is your area of concern as you work on increasing your personal command power to its maximum. This chapter is designed to give you techniques for using power psychology to that end.

After years of study, there are still some unanswered questions about psychology and its many applications, but we do know that power psychology can be used with astounding success.

THE EXTRA STEP THAT ADDS TO YOUR PCP

We have no intention of engaging in any psychobabble since we are only interested in the practical application of psychology. With this in mind, a few more observations are in order regarding the nature and techniques of power psychology.

First of all, power psychology deals with the subconscious as well as the conscious. The subconscious mental processes outweigh the conscious ones, both numerically and quantitatively. The subconscious receives a network of impressions, reactions, commands, and associations, all of which determine the individual's response to power. As you lead, motivate, push, and control others in the field of subconscious psychology, you will win cooperation without undue resistance.

Power psychology is not a cut and dried body of facts and formulas, and it really has meaning for you because it is a tool of command power. Since your mind is psychoactive, whatever enters your brain produces action, because it is the place where power psychology gets its start.

TECHNIQUES FOR ESTABLISHING PSYCHOLOGICAL POWER THAT WINS

1. Confront obstacles.

It is sound psychology to confront obstacles promptly because delay only prolongs the agony. For example, if you have a competitor or an opponent standing in your way, facing him with boldness and confidence will give you the psychological advantage. When you walk right up and look an opponent in the eye, he most likely will think he has underestimated you; this in itself is an advantage that opens the way for you to pour on the power psychology.

Tell your opponent you know where he stands, then restate your position. Tell him that you can respect his thinking, but that you cannot permit him to stand in your way. Let him know that you are prepared to listen to anything within reason, but that nothing will swerve you from your course. Then, if you can do so without revealing any secret strategies, explain how and why you will win, and smile and shake hands if possible. If not, ignore the cries of outrage and surprise and go ahead with your program as one smart salesman did.

Pete Feldman had obtained a new item with which to round out his line of small appliances. However, he had an obstacle to overcome in the town of Harrison because Charles Ashmore of City Home Products would consider no more new items, even though he insisted on being Pete's account exclusively. Pete walked in with the new item, and explained that although he could understand Mr. Ashmore's position, he had another hot new appliance that nevertheless had to be placed in Harrison that day. When Mr. Ashmore still balked, Pete picked up his sample saying that he would like to have Mr. Ashmore's cooperation but if not, he was obliged to take his new merchandise to Mr. Ashmore's competition, Modern Home Appliances. With that, Mr. Ashmore threatened to quit buying at all, and Pete said, "Gee, I'm sorry. That wouldn't do either of us any good. But since you won't stock this new item, you leave me no choice." When Pete started for the door again, Mr. Ashmore called him back with, "I think I can find room for it if you really feel that way about it."

Pete had made the most of applied power psychology: he acknowledged Mr. Ashmore's right to disagree, stated his own position, refused to be swayed, and stuck with his plan. Without a doubt, Modern Home Appliances would definitely have had the new appliance if Mr. Ashmore had not agreed to cooperate. But fortunately, Pete's adroit use of power psychology made him and his old friend winners, and Mr. Ashmore is pleased that the new appliance is one of his best-selling units.

2. Protect your helpers.

When you employ power psychology to win support, your helpers have the right to expect your protection. This makes sense, because if you use your psychopower to demean or destroy others, they will be of little use to you. So, once you have won agreement and cooperation, you sustain your own growing power by protecting the interests of your helpers. Since only strong, working helpers benefit you, when they cooperate, you must protect them in much the same way that salesman Pete Feldman did when he used power psychology to sway his customer. He continued to work with Charles Ashmore exclusively after achieving an agreement with him, thus protecting his helper from more competition while, at the same time, strengthening his own position. This psychological power keeps your winning strategy intact.

3. Project personal power.

When you project personal power, you pave the way for establishing winning psychological power. You project this power by acting and speaking with confidence. Make your actions so definite that no one can question your motives or intent. Back this up with assertive sentences like the following:

- This is the way it is going to be done.
- This is a dynamic opportunity.
- The quicker we get into action, the sooner the money rolls in.
- Be here at 8 in the morning.
- Don't hand this to somebody else.
- Save money by acting today.
- There will never be a better time.
- You can't lose.
- The facts are here for you to see.
- I can show you how.

Positive action and assertive speech are two prime ingredients in projecting personal power and winning agreement and cooperation.

4. Spell it out.

When you are conducting a campaign to establish psychological win-power, it is of paramount importance that your helpers understand exactly what you are proposing. Since they will want to know what is in it for them you will have to dangle the apple. The following case illustrates how this technique can be applied.

Steve Vestall, sales manager for an industrial electrical manufacturing concern, had been given the assignment of increasing sales by $1,000,000 over a six-month period. He himself had also been promised a 2 percent incentive override if this quota was met. Steve then called a meeting of the firm's ten territory salesmen to explain the situation. After delineating the proposal, he held up his hand to silence the moans and described the increased advertising budget that management had approved. Then he showed them the new sales kits especially prepared for the drive. In addition, he said, a billing extension of thirty days would be given to accounts with solid credit, and as the clincher, he told them a 2 percent bonus would go to each man who exceeded the $100,000 extra quota assigned him. Steve's final shot of power psychology was the assurance that any man who failed to meet his quota during the campaign would have his total performance reevaluated to determine his qualifications for continued employment.

It is easy to see that Steve used forceful procedures: *he* laid the program before the men, *he* stifled premature objection, and *he* explained the back-up work that had been done. Then, after he had told his helpers exactly what was proposed, he told them what was in it for them. His power statement regarding the reevaluation of anyone failing to give full support was added psycho-power that spelled out his determination to win. While he dangled the extra 2 percent bonus for each salesman who produced, he kept a tight grip on the deal since he did not mention his own 2 percent bonus on the whole ball of wax.

5. Break opposition into smaller units.

When you face opposition, put your power quickly to work by breaking your opposition into manageable units. This is a workable technique to establish winning psychological power. When opposition comes at you like an avalanche, decide who is orchestrating the opposition, then go to work on him. Once you get the chief troublemaker to see the light of reason, you will have little trouble disposing of the other parts of the problem and you don't have to take on a whole mob at once. When you break the problem into smaller units by accosting one opponent at a time, you can go through the ranks, handling a formidable group one at a time.

Donald Miller, the new young branch manager for a national merchandising firm, was having problems with four senior employees who resented his youth and ambition. It was obvious to Don that the ringleader was one Ellis Dixon, so Don took Mr. Dixon out for a cup of coffee. He got to the point by telling Dixon that he was aware of the problem that he and his three cohorts were creating with their sarcasm, griping, and slipshod work. "Now," he said, "there is no way that all four of you could have this job, but if you cooperate in making this an outstanding branch, you can be promoted to just about any position you are qualified to fill. I am going to put this branch on top, and I would like to do it with your help. But if not, I can handle it. If you show up for work tomorrow, I will take that as indication of your full agreement and we will go on from there. And since you have been the leader in this misguided attack against me, it will now be your job to straighten the other three men out. That is your first assignment for tomorrow."

Ellis Dixon was on time the next morning, and he did get the word to the other three. The atmosphere cleared immediately and the branch moved forward. By breaking the opposition into smaller units, Donald Miller established a firm base for the continued use of his considerable psychological power. At the same time, he wiped out the organized opposition of the whole group.

When you face opposition, work on it one day at a time and one unit at a time; it's good psychology.

6. Never compromise yourself.

This is self-explanatory. But you can use the following pointers to insure that this will never be one of your power problems.

- Don't move until you are prepared to win.
- Act promptly and decisively.
- Keep your word.
- Establish realistic goals.
- Command respect from the start.
- Motivate your helpers.
- Inspire great expectations.
- Be sure your orders and instructions are understood.
- Use psychology as a personal power tool.

These points will automatically become part of your personal power when you use the techniques you have and will study in this book. Remember, the firmer the base you build for your psychological power, the more effective your personal winning techniques will become.

POWER PSYCHOLOGY IS MORE THAN POPULARITY

Popularity is an indication of social acceptance, but it is not necessarily an indication of power. When you meet someone who seems to have the admiration of everybody in the world, ask yourself why. Is it because he or she is so powerful that universal adoration is spontaneous? Not likely. More probably, he or she makes few demands, tolerates circumstances instead of shaping them, and has limited ambition.

Popularity is not a vice, but it is more important to be a creative, productive leader than it is to be the person with the toothiest smile. Be popular if you can, but do it while commanding respect and cooperation. This calls for psychological power, and if you have to make a choice between personal power and popularity, power will do more for you and those you motivate to follow you.

On more than one occasion, I have heard a sales manager with a tough self-image announce to a room of salesmen, "I'm not here to win a popularity contest." This bare-knuckle approach may irritate some people, but it does serve a purpose. It makes it crystal clear that the sales manager is more interested in results than in warm little pats on the back. This is the attitude of psychological power.

In this matter of popularity versus psycho-power, it is far better to be candid with your helpers than to lie. Nobody worth his salt wants to be flattered constantly. And what is to be gained by telling someone that he is more intelligent, competent, or capable than he really is? If you tell someone he is doing remarkably well on a project, yet he sees others doing far better work, the logical assumption will be that you are less than honest or don't know what you are talking about. It doesn't take much imagination to see what this can do to your power.

The better way to exert psychological power is to candidly state exactly what you believe, want, and expect. This can be done without rejecting or maiming your helper. Explain that you recognize the contribution he has made on your behalf, reemphasize what you want, and show him how to be more proficient. This will benefit *you*, both psychologically and materially.

Forceful honesty is the integral part of power psychology that wins agreement and cooperation.

HOW TO BE COURTEOUS BUT FIRM

Watching somebody be polite to the point of obsequiousness is about as exciting as watching a can rust. Psychological power is not servile, and although it is possible and desirable to be courteous, you must also be firm. And the emphasis here is on *firm*.

As you begin to use your psychology to win, one of the first things you will discover is that all people are full of self-doubts. Because of this, they seldom use their own power and ability to get things done because working below one's level is easy and comfortable. Therefore, as a power leader, your goal is to jar them into doing their best for you without making them gun-shy. Common courtesy will reassure them, and firmness will propel them forward.

At a seminar on job satisfaction, I watched a skilled market-ing man convince a group of middle-level managers and train-ees both to endorse his ideas, and to fully commit themselves to reaching the high standards he set for them. After outlining company goals and stressing the responsibility of individual performance, he passed out plain white 3"×5" cards. Then he instructed each person to list the six things he most wanted from his job. This done, he asked each man to turn his card face down on the table. Now he applied psychological power by linking company goals with individual employee goals. He instructed the participants to turn the cards over and scratch off the two items least important to them. This done, he explained that the individual should focus on what he really wanted, then scratch off the *next* two least important items.

As soon as each man had done this, he had them stand one by one and read the two most important items left on their cards. Almost without exception, the goals selected by this process were "money" and "recognition."

After a dramatic pause, the leader demanded, "Is there any better way to get what you want than by giving the best to your job?"

The point had been made with firmness and power, yet nobody was hurt. The end result was improved morale and superior performance because each individual saw that it was possible for him to get what he wanted, and the powerful executive also had what *he* wanted: full agreement and coopera-tion.

PEOPLE TAKE ADVANTAGE OF "MR. SUGAR"

They may love him, but people take advantage of a "Mr. Sugar." And why not? He is asking for it.

We are not suggesting that you abandon courtesy since

there is no gain in being rude. But there is danger in convincing yourself that you must be sweet in every situation. Some situations demand forceful behavior, and some people only respond to forceful action. To such characters, sugary behavior is a sign of weakness, so smile often, but not always. Personal charm may endear you to those who love favors, but it takes power to win.

Bob Hilken learned the cost of a perpetual smile when he was skipped over for a promotion to department head by a man with less experience. When Bob complained to his superior, he explained that Bob had been considered, but that the job required a tough disciplinarian. When Bob insisted on knowing what made him think he couldn't handle it, his superior told him that his smile and overly-solicitous manner would have been a handicap in controlling strong-willed employees. That was when Bob's smile vanished. He can still smile, but he is no longer "Mr. Sugar," since he still wants to become a department head.

Being sweet may be good psychology given the right time and circumstances, but psychological power gets more done where it counts.

WHAT HAPPENED WHEN DON PERKINS DROPPED HIS "MR. SUGAR" ROLE

Don Perkins, an obliging employee in the accounting department of a growing firm, was made office manager. As a bookkeeper minding his own business, Don was affable, solicitous, and genial but this carried over into his new executive position. Soon, however, Don was forced to admit that office production was slipping. This was primarily because the office employees were making the most of Don's benign attitude by taking longer coffee breaks than the fifteen minutes allotted twice a day, and were stretching lunch hours far beyond the one hour limit. Finally, the old manager called Don aside and cautioned him, "You will never make it that way. The office force will love you for being so sweet, but they'll kill you in the process. You had better take charge while you still have the option!"

Don had never crossed anyone before in his life, but the next morning, he called a ten-minute meeting. He even surprised himself when he resolutely demanded strict adherence to company policy regarding coffee breaks and lunch periods. Then he wound up his statement of authority by observing that if there was anyone in the group who could not tell time, then he or she was totally unsuited for the exacting work expected in his office.

Don believes that this one outspoken exhibition of psychological power has done more for office efficiency than anything since the computer.

WHY PEOPLE AGREE AND COOPERATE
WITH STRONG LEADERS

Put bluntly, people agree and cooperate with strong leaders because they do not want the responsibilities of leadership. Further, the vast majority are looking for leaders who will pay the price of success for them!

As a strong leader, you can apply psychological power to take full advantage of this all too common feeling. Your opportunity to lead is great, and the following reasons explain why people agree with and cooperate with commanding leaders.

1. The leader relieves them of personal responsibility.
2. They want to identify with strong leaders.
3. The leader makes decisions for them.
4. The leader takes the risks; when he wins, they win, if he loses, they are still where they were.
5. The leader protects them because he is the authority figure.
6. The leader provides ideas and inspiration.
7. The leader fights their battles while they cheer from the sidelines.
8. The leader can say "no" for them.

9. The leader is the boss.
10. People like to be bossed.

This idea should reinforce your determination to do what is needed to become a leader: when you motivate, prod, push, inspire, and use people in a productive way, you are doing them a favor. To say the least, you will never put anybody on the welfare rolls when you apply power psychology to make them productive.

Finally, you do not owe happiness to anyone. Too often happiness is looked upon as the absence of work and responsibility. But making people happy using sugar-coated behavior is not the goal of power psychology. The purpose of power psychology is to obtain cooperation to get what you want.

INSTANT POWER POINTERS

- Power psychology can be used with astounding success.
- Power psychology is a tool of command power.
- To establish winning psychological power you must:

     1. Confront obstacles promptly.
     2. Protect your helpers.
     3. Project personal power.
     4. Spell it out clearly.
     5. Break the opposition into smaller units.
     6. Never compromise yourself.

- Power psychology is more than popularity.
- You can be courteous and firm at the same time.
- People take advantage of "Mr. Sugar" types.
- You do not owe happiness to anyone.

16

How to Deal with
the First Person Singular Syndrome

Self-image and self-confidence are prerequisites of personal command power. This is sufficient reason to take a close look at the first person singular syndrome.

THE FIRST PERSON SINGULAR SYNDROME DEFINED

First person singular refers to the "I" and "me," and considers only one person. The syndrome can be explained as a pattern of symptoms (emotions or actions) that indicate a particular abnormality or fear. The first person singular syndrome, as it pertains to command power, consists of being too concerned with the thousand and one things that might adversely affect you. It is, however, something that can be handled and controlled. Therefore this examination of the problem is designed to enable anyone interested in power and authority to quickly identify and wipe out the first signs of it. It is also useful in developing the capacity to identify this syndrome in others. Now, when you see that someone you are trying to motivate or manipulate is suffering from too much anxiety over the future, you will be in a position to placate him or to apply more pressure, whichever you may deem appropriate.

The following list of questions is constructed to give you a picture of the agonizing doubts suffered by someone afflicted with the first person singular syndrome. Such misgivings are apparent in questions such as:

- What will happen to me?
- What if I fail?
- What will others think of me?
- What if they don't like it?
- Will I get hurt?
- Will I lose face?
- Can I handle resistance?
- What if they laugh at me?
- How can I be sure?
- Will I chicken out at the last minute?

Diagnosis is the first step in correcting the problem. Questions such as these are the symptoms of the first person singular syndrome. By their nature, such questions show an excessive amount of self-concern while little thought is given to achieving positive results. This is contrary to power thinking, which regards results as first and foremost.

To put such symptomatic questions into proper perspective, consider the following factual items.

Fact #1: Every winner loses sometimes.

There are two damaging misconceptions about losing: one, that we must win at all costs, and two, that there is something dreadfully wrong with us if and when we lose.

The man or woman filled with command power pursues every goal with all the means at his or her disposal. Yet, all the while, ambitious, power-driven individuals know that it is winning the war that counts, not winning every encounter no matter how meaningless it may be in relation to their goals. If, after suffering a temporary setback, you find yourself enraged, frus-

trated, immobilized, depressed, angry, or condemning yourself, then you are making yourself a victim. Look at it this way:
an occasional failure is a natural and necessary part of the de-
velopment of PCP. Your total success is not predicated on never
losing.

There were two young accountants taking the examination
which would qualify them as Certified Public Accountants. Both
failed. Jack Gross, one of the candidates, threw his hands up in
anger and despair, vowing that he would have nothing more to
do with a profession that treated him so badly. He was as good
as his threat—and no better! At last report, Jack Gross was
selling ladies shoes in a retail store. While there is nothing
wrong with selling ladies shoes, in Mr. Gross's case, it made him
miserable and depressed working in a field that made little use
of his considerable talents.

Meanwhile, Francis Koch, the other aspiring CPA, exercised sound judgment and personal power. He resolved to
prepare himself better and be ready for the next examination.
Today he is a practicing CPA.

One man gave up after losing a battle: he is still immobilized
and unhappy, all because he abandoned the fight when he lost
the first round. However, the other man is enjoying money,
prestige, and satisfaction. Such are the fruits of victory for those
who accept the fact that every winner is subject to losing occasionally. This attitude, coupled with a determination to learn
and profit from the experience, will win the war.

Fact #2: One lost skirmish does not wipe out PCP.

PCP is as tough and enduring as granite. It anticipates
problems, annoying delays, opposition, possible localized loss,
and disappointment along the way. Command power stacks up
reserves and options for just such emergencies.

With PCP, when you prepare for the possibility of a lost
skirmish, you can face it with equanimity. The dictionary definition of equanimity aptly emphasizes the importance of such
preparation: "*Equanimity*, 1: Evenness of mind especially under
stress. 2: Right disposition; 3: The characteristic quality of one
who is self-possessed and not easily disturbed or perturbed."

It will be a rare occasion when you launch a program to

motivate and control people without advance thought and planning. Let a contingency plan be part of your strategy. This positions you to handle any lost skirmishes with equanimity as you keep pressing to win. Further, this positive attitude will keep the first person singular syndrome in the shade.

Fact #3: Bouncing back after defeat is a sign of personal command power.

Bouncing back after being unceremoniously flattened is a convincing sign of power. Nothing discourages opposition more than watching a strong person get up and plow back into the fray time after time, and nothing will come closer to guaranteeing eventual success than bouncing back after defeat. For ideas to build bouncing back power, see Fact #2 again.

Fact #4: You should be glad for rivals.

Rivals and competitors have no magic tricks or techniques: they are subject to the same laws and limitations as you. The only time a rival or competitor has an unearned advantage is when you accord him power that exists only in your imagination. An abnormal dread or fear of rivalry is often due to a low self-respect level regarding your own capabilities and power. This is one more example of the first person singular syndrome: too much emphasis on "I."

The following are just a few reasons why you should be grateful for rivalry and competition.

- A rival keeps you on your toes.
- A rival jars you out of your rut.
- Competition and rivalry force you to keep up-to-date.
- Rivalry inspires you to try harder.
- Rivalry keeps your skills and techniques sharp.
- A rival or competitor keeps your power boiling.
- Competition adds spice and excitement to winning.

One successful independent insurance broker says that a rival actually doubled his business for him, as the next example shows.

Dale Armiger had been coasting along quite comfortably in his insurance agency until one morning when he found that an aggressive competitor had moved into the same building where Armiger had his offices. His first reaction was anger and panic, but Mr. Armiger was no novice at power games. He promptly hired two more bright salesmen and began spending more time in the field himself. After six months, the rival moved out while Armiger Insurance kept up the momentum spurred by the rival. At year's end, Armiger's business had doubled, and Mr. Armiger gives his competitor much of the credit.

When faced with a rival, do what Mr. Armiger did: turn on the juice. Then you can be glad for rivals just as Armiger Insurance found out.

Fact #5: PCP can put you in charge of your competition and your problems.

Basically this is because when you are involved in applying your winning power, you are not fragmenting yourself with worry over the outcome. In this setting, you are too busy *making* things happen to worry. You are concentrating on results.

How this works is illustrated by the story of two salesmen working for the same company. One failed miserably by exhausting himself with worry about what the competition was selling and about the problems the competitor might cause him. The other took the attitude that since he didn't have the competitor's merchandise to sell, he would not worry about it. Rather, he put his energy and power into selling the goods he did have for sale. And, if he did it well, he figured, the competition would be no problem. Naturally, this man became his firm's star salesman.

Fact #6: PCP puts the first person singular syndrome in its place.

The place in which the first person singular syndrome belongs is where it cannot weaken your power. This, of course, means putting it out of your mind, and the way to do this with anything troublesome as psychologists have long maintained, is to keep busy with stronger, healthier projects. So, concentrate your PCP on getting what you want and motivating people to help you get what you want. By turning your power on with PCP ideas and techniques, you will put the first person singular syndrome in its place.

HOW TO ISOLATE AND OVERCOME COMPONENTS OF THE SYNDROME

Healthy, aggressive behavior is based on the belief that we have just as much power as our contemporaries, or more. Unless we exercise this capability advantageously, our opinion of our own power decreases. This leads to dangerous misgivings and doubts, which in turn, can degenerate into a form of "me-ism" that dissipates power through a defensive, self-protective attitude. This type of a protective posture does not lend itself to power action.

As you deal objectively with the first person singular syndrome, this need never happen to you. By breaking the syndrome into its components, it becomes easier to understand it and deal with it. Consider these:

● Hostility

Hostility is a normal physiological response to power. When you pile pressure on others, you can also feel it directed toward yourself by those who resent authority figures. But you can handle this form of hostility since it is out in the open where you can meet it head-on with all the power techniques at your disposal. However, the hostility that breeds the first person singular syndrome is much more difficult to handle, and is also more deadly because it is directed toward you by yourself. This often happens when an ambitious, intelligent human being fails to use the power at his or her command, because he or she fears what might happen. A poor self-image causes hostility toward one's self, which in turn, further lowers self-esteem and promotes the sorry self-image.

How do you overcome this hostility which you direct at yourself? Such platitudes as "put on a happy face," "Smile," or "just forget all about yourself," won't work. Instead, try these suggestions from the experts.

First of all, isolate the problem and admit that what you feel is really hostility toward yourself. It is sheer folly to hide or suppress such a feeling: it won't fool you and it certainly won't fool anyone else.

Then, once you have diagnosed your suppressed self-hostility and conquered it, you will discover that you are indeed a person with power, but that you have not been applying all of it toward achieving your goals and motivating others to help you attain them. The secret here is to boldly put your power into action in the many ways we have and will study. As I once read, no problem was ever solved without action, and the problem of self-hostility is no exception: the answer lies within you.

Earl Denny had been ordered to see the company psychologist because his supervisor had told him to find out what was bugging him or else turn in his resignation. The interview went as follows:

> **Psychologist:** "Why are you so hostile?"
>
> **Earl:** "But I am not hostile."
>
> **Psychologist:** "Well, your supervisor says you are."
>
> **Earl:** "I don't care what my supervisor says."
>
> **Psychologist:** "How do you really feel about the supervisor?"
>
> **Earl:** "He's no good. He gave John Timmons the promotion I should have had."
>
> **Psychologist:** "The supervisor has to be fair. What would you have done had you been in his place?"
>
> **Earl,** looking sober and crestfallen: "The same thing, I guess."

From that point it was easy for the psychologist to show Earl that his hostility was really directed at himself because he had failed to prepare for the promotion he could have had. When Earl isolated the problem and identified and faced it with the help of the psychologist, he was able to rid himself of this handicap. Soon he regained his self-respect by putting his PCP back to work, and is now a dedicated employee who is taking company-sponsored evening courses designed to assure his progress. He will shortly be directing other employees who, in turn, will push him even further up the ladder.

Recognizing self-hostility and taking action against it as Earl did, is an effective way to deal with this sneaky syndrome.

● Anxiety

Anxiety is pain, and like most pain it has a cause. But, unlike transient pain, such as when you stub your toe or bang your thumb with a hammer, the cause of anxiety is difficult to uncover. This is because anxiety is a reaction to a preconceived condition, and in the case of those of us who keenly desire power and competence, this preconceived notion most likely stems from discontent with ourselves because we have not taken action. Anxiety is distracting, and it interferes with concentration and action, thereby obscuring our abilities and power.

There is no easy remedy for removing anxiety. However, the best way to come to grips with it is by going tooth and nail after something you want. Then, when you are busy guiding and directing people, you will have no time for the self-concern that feeds anxiety.

For five years, Alan Benstock talked about how he was going to open his own real estate brokerage business. But then he would always add, "There are so many factors to consider." This statement revealed Alan's overriding anxiety about what might happen to him. Finally, an exasperated friend commented: "When you stop talking and squirming about it, then we will believe you are actually going to do it."

This challenge awakened Alan: he did go into business, and he was highly successful. When he isolated his anxiety and fought his way out of it, his power took over. He now has the respect, prestige, security, and money that he worried about for so long. This worry had prevented him from taking action.

Like Alan, you will gain the following benefits by isolating and dealing with anxiety:

1. You will no longer worry.
2. You will build self-confidence.

3. Others will respect you.
4. Your prestige will be high.
5. You will earn security.
6. You will earn good money.
7. People will cooperate with you.
8. Your power will grow.

● Superman complex

Superman exists only in the movies, TV, and comic strips. Remember: you don't have to be a superman to exert your power. In fact, the people you would like to direct and use will cooperate more readily with a regular, strong, healthy individual than they ever would with someone having a superman complex. It is therefore a mistake to wait until you believe you are stronger than anybody in the world before putting your PCP to work. Instead, start with what you have. Then you can have all the benefits Alan Benstock reaped when he finally worked with what he had, in the existing circumstances.

One more hint: don't think of an opponent or competitor as a superman. What does he have, really, that you don't?

● The martyr complex

Since you are obviously interested in exercising PCP, it is highly unlikely that you will ever suffer from the martyr complex. But, for enlightenment, let's examine how the martyr complex works. An able individual who has the training, skill, and ability to use his power to accomplish a great deal, will rationalize about the terrible obstacles he faces. His rationale convinces him that he is not to blame if his personal power fizzles. Consequently, he leaves to someone else the prestigious job, the money, the respect, and all the other factors that go with putting command power to work. Undoubtedly, this attitude is greatly appreciated by his rivals.

My philosophy regarding the martyr complex prohibits my feeling sympathy for such an individual. It is foolish to be a powerless martyr, since nobody appreciates the martyr while he is here and probably even less after he is gone.

HOW TO DEAL WITH THE SYNDROME
IN BUSINESS

Your job, business, or profession can be a source of great satisfaction. However, it can't if the first person singular syndrome is filling you with apprehension about future disasters. Personal command power is an absolute in the business world, just as in the business of life.

The first person singular syndrome—too much emphasis on me and what might conceivably harm me—can go from one extreme to the other. It can either cause the victim to withdraw in fear and apprehension to the point where he is practically out of the race, or it can cause this self-chosen victim to become hostile and suspicious toward every business activity or friend involved.

Salesmen and sales executives frequently wind up in the hospital as a result of suppressed hostility that they are not even aware they possess. There are often many reasons for this syndrome. The salesman is often caught between customers who pressure him for better service, faster shipments, lower prices, and are prone to holding the competition over the salesman's head. Or on the other end, the sales manager may always be demanding more and more sales. This catches the sales executive between two fires. The upper echelon managers expect and demand so much from the sales manager. Yet, if he, in turn harasses the salesmen, he may lose good men. Soon all parties feel that they are being treated unfairly, and the hostility boils. The results are never good. If hostility flares out in the open and wild exchanges take place, jobs are lost and turmoil adds to the problem. But if it is suppressed, the victim can end up ill, and even in the hospital. This hostility chain reaction is not limited to the sales department. The same unrelenting pressure can move through the ranks of all departments in all businesses.

The knee-jerk reaction to a business wrong, real or imagined, is to strike back regardless of the cost. But there are better ways to deal with business problems, and even if you work in a boiler-room atmosphere, you can still avoid the first person singular problem. Instead of withdrawing or committing mayhem (chiefly to yourself) you can put your PCP to work on avoiding business hostility. Use the following measures to head off the first person singular syndrome's symptoms and agony.

• Admit a mistake if you make one, and realize that it's doubly important to confess our mistakes to ourselves. When we admit a mistake, the way is cleared for correcting the error without additional stress and strain.

• Leave the other fellow a few shreds of self-respect. If he has made a mistake, even if the mistake was in taking you on as a competitor or opponent, when you let him save face after putting him in place, he won't spend a lot of time baying angrily at your heels.

• Don't look upon every business reprimand as a personal insult. The pressures of business are such that blunt actions and blunt words are to be expected occasionally. This is not the way it should be according to psychologists, but it happens often, so don't let it bruise your power.

• Keep in mind that although blowing your top might relieve a little pressure, it is not a good way to win in the business world. Use your energy to motivate and guide people, not to knock heads with them.

• Work actively at risk-taking: this is the ultimate answer to the first person syndrome. Lay down ground rules for your own behavior because motivating, guiding, prompting, using, and influencing people is a calculated risk, like many other business activities. As you make it yor business to take this most important risk (working with and through people on a personal power basis) you will never be afflicted with that power-robber, the first person singular syndrome.

As for becoming withdrawn in fear and apprehension, individuals like yourself with command power and personal accomplishment on their minds will never give anyone enough power over them to push them into this unhappy state. Command power will not allow you to be victimized.

INSTANT POWER POINTERS

• The first person singular syndrome is an abnormal concern with the "I" and the "Me."

- Diagnosis and recognition is the first step toward correcting the problem.
- Personal command power can put the syndrome in its place.
- Breaking the syndrome into its components makes it easier to understand and to deal with.
- Components to watch carefully are:

    Hostility
    Self-hostility
    Anxiety
    The superman complex

- The syndrome can cause knee-jerk reactions in business.
- Actively working at risk-taking routs the syndrome.
- Command power does not allow you to be victimized into withdrawal.

17

How to Handle the Belligerent Character

The worthless and offensive members of society,
whose existence is a social pest, invariably think themselves
the most ill-used people alive, and never get over their
astonishment at the ingratitude and selfishness of their
contemporaries.

—*Ralph Waldo Emerson*

Not every belligerent uncooperative person that you meet
will fall into Ralph Waldo Emerson's powerful indictment.
However, there are enough belligerents around who *do* belong
in this category that you should keep this observation in mind.

Much of the belligerence in our social and business worlds
can be attributed to just such a lack of understanding as Emerson's "worthless and offensive members" exhibit.

But our purpose here is not to arbitrarily label anyone.
Rather, we wish to promote an understanding and appreciation
of the validity and uses of personal power. Keep this truth in
mind as you apply your personal command power to motivate
and move people: if there is any way for you to be misunderstood, you will be misunderstood, and by every belligerent
character you meet.

HOW TO AVOID BEING
GROSSLY MISUNDERSTOOD BY THE BELLIGERENT

We use the term "grossly misunderstood" to emphasize that you cannot avoid all misunderstandings. Anybody who does, or even so much as tries to, is still going to be misunderstood upon occasion. But this is no cause for self-flagellation. Belligerent characters are often not even remotely interested in objective understanding. Rather, due to a shaky self-image, they will oppose command power on any flimsy excuse. This is a major problem of those who indulge in bellicose behavior. With them, your concern is to avoid being grossly misunderstood, and the following secret techniques will serve you well.

● Don't pull your punches.

When you are forcefully engaged in an undertaking, don't soft-pedal it. Should you use balmy speech or try to charm your helpers, you will only get clobbered by the belligerent dissident. He will misunderstand your concern, which will be interpreted by him as indecisiveness or weakness, and will only encourage his senseless resistance. Use bold, convincing, to-the-point language. Hammer home what you expect from each helper. This will avoid gross misunderstandings and the belligerent will be sure to get the correct message.

Another power note on this technique: it will work as effectively in a one-on-one confrontation as it will when you address a group that you are determined to move at your direction.

● Repeat—repeat—repeat!

Emphatic repetition of instructions is a secret technique often employed by strong motivators to avoid misunderstandings. Each repetition is actually like a hammer blow to the brain and, in fact, the human brain quickly grasps and retains things which are repeated. Instructions, directives, or orders that are mentioned only once are not only likely to be misunderstood; instead they will be forgotten. Repeat what you want often. Nobody will become bored or inattentive if you do it forcefully and with variety.

For example, John Clayton, sales manager for State Frozen Foods, had decided that he wanted a hundred new accounts within a month. He began his speech outlining his plan to the twelve-man sales force in this way:

"This meeting has been called because each man here must open ten new accounts this month. We have the price and the quality products each of you needs to get your ten new accounts within the next thirty days. Holding up a specials sheet he said, "Here are the offers that will make it easy for you to open ten new accounts this month."

John repeated the "ten new accounts" theme to them throughout the sales meeting. There was no misunderstanding, as is evidenced by the one hundred and thirty-one new accounts which were opened during those thirty days.

Repeat—repeat—repeat! This will emphasize and make clear what you want, will avoid gross misunderstandings, and will give the belligerent very little room in which to maneuver.

- **Highlight benefits for your helpers.**

No matter how belligerent and difficult a prospective helper may be, he still wants to know how he will benefit by doing as you say. Therefore, highlight the benefits for the hardhead. If the insurgent thinks he will get something out of your deal, the fire of understanding will light in his bosom. The fire will burn even more brightly if he also understands what he will forfeit if he insists on playing the sulking game.

Joe Scammon, a rugged old millionaire twice over, had made most of his money manufacturing men's work clothes. It was his policy to pay only minimum wages and to provide as little job comfort as possible. Obviously this made it difficult for his foreman to keep the machines manned, but the straw that broke the camel's back was an abrupt memo from Scammon stating that the women operators' two ten-minute coffee breaks were to be terminated at once. Naturally the women screamed at Dave Lynch, the foreman, so Dave made up his mind to use his muscle on the belligerent owner. The operators agreed to back him all the way, and Dave approached old Joe. "Mr. Scammon," he began, "I am reinstating the coffee breaks as of now."

"The blankety-blank you are! I'm running this outfit," growled his boss.

"I understand that, and I'm trying to help. If we reinstate the coffee breaks, production will be kept on schedule and we can deliver those eastern orders as contracted," explained Dave.

"And what happens if I don't? Seems to me cutting out those coffee breaks would speed up production," grumped Mr. Scammon.

"What happens if you don't, is that you will be here tomorrow by yourself. That is, except for the pickets outside demanding a lot more than coffee breaks. Think about it," replied the foreman.

"And another thing," Dave threw in, "the first of the month is when you promised the women a raise."

Mr. Scammon sputtered, but Dave had gotten his point across to his belligerent employer. Scammon now understood what he had to gain by his positive response, and he also understood what he could lose by his recalcitrance. He nodded agreement and Dave took the ball from there. The machines kept humming, and Dave followed up by reminding Mr. Scammon to institute the promised pay raise: it came through on time.

- **Don't apologize to the opposition.**

As has been indicated, an individual who exercises power is going to have to battle some opposition from time to time. Of course the belligerent character will always be in the forefront of any such opposition since it is his nature. Because he feels insecure and inferior, the chronic belligerent is constantly looking for a scapegoat who relieves him of having to face his personality problem. When he tries to place the guilt on somebody else, he shifts the attention from his own shortcomings. So do not heed the falsetto cries of outrage from such opposition as this, and do not apologize for your power. If you do, the belligerent will grossly misunderstand and will interpret your apology as surrender.

EXPECT TO MEET A BELLIGERENT CHARACTER

Harmony should be your goal as you work to make your command power more and more productive. But you must expect to meet a belligerent person occasionally since they exist in social settings, in families, in the business arena, and wherever there are people. So be prepared to handle the belligerent: everybody bumps into him once in awhile.

When Phil Curran agreed to take over a lucrative sales territory for Greenwald Sales and Promotions, he had every reason to expect harmony and cooperation. Fortunately, he had the experience and power for dealing with belligerents, because he was soon put to the test.

After interviews in Greenwald's home office where he was hired, Phil was sent to meet Kenneth Hughes, a regional manager who was to indoctrinate him. Phil met Hughes in a fashionable restaurant at his request, and listened respectfully to a rather belligerent outline of his duties and the company policies. Then, when dinner was over and he was through with his discourse, Hughes announced in his most magnanimous manner that since he was the boss, he was going to the best hotel in town. He condescendingly explained that he had made reservations for Phil at a third-rate hotel. It was at this point that Phil's command power surfaced. He told Mr. Hughes he had given Phil the impression that Greenwald's was a first-rate concern. If he was to be treated as a second-rate citizen his employment was over then and there. Mr. Hughes' antagonistic attitude withered. He mumbled something about holding down expenses, but promptly phoned to get a room for Phil at the choice hotel. The men never became close friends, but they worked as equals. That is, for one year: then Phil was promoted over his egocentric co-worker's head.

Since you are almost certain to meet an occasional belligerent character, the following questionnaire is designed to help you determine how well prepared you are to deal with the situation. Do not be dismayed if you miss a question or two. The purpose of this questionnaire is not to grade you, but to pinpoint areas that you may want to reinforce.

When you meet a belligerent character, do you:

1. Become angry?
2. Out shout the antagonist?
3. Ignore the belligerent?

4. Make concessions?

5. Stand your ground?

6. Emphasize why it is to the belligerent's advantage to cooperate?

7. Tell the belligerent how you can manage with or without him?

8. Make threats?

9. Detail the benefits that the belligerent may expect by cooperation?

10. Do exactly what you tell the antagonist you're going to do?

11. Keep your dignity?

12. Refuse to deviate from your original program or plan?

If you answer yes to numbers 1, 2, 3, 4, 8, this indicates that you are subconsciously being manipulated by the belligerent, since these items describe defensive tactics. Numbers 5, 6, 7, 9, 10, 11, 12 are power postures, so these items embrace the determination that will win. Channel your command power along these lines to establish your authority over a belligerent opponent.

HOW PERSONAL COMMAND POWER SPARES YOU FRUSTRATION AND EMBARRASSMENT

When you use personal command power to handle a misguided belligerent, you not only do him a favor by screwing his head on right, but you also spare yourself considerable frustration and embarrassment. Trying to deal with the habitual belligerent on the basis of reason alone is usually futile because if he were a reasonable man, he would not be chronically belligerent. The ideas in the questionnaire just presented can help you, and you can add these ideas to your forceful personality and to the techniques you have learned and will soon develop. This will spare you much frustration and embarrassment when you must lock horns with this type of unhappy individual. The cases that follow illustrate the validity of this principle.

Pamela Frank, a teetotaler married to a successful, beer loving attorney, had an annoying problem with her belligerent husband. At his office, where he worked congenially with three other attorneys and a contingent of clerks and secretaries, his manners were impeccable. However, at home he left his empty beer cans sitting on the furniture, or on the floor, much to the embarrassment and chagrin of his wife. In addition, when Pam, a meticulous housekeeper, asked her husband to dispose of his empties in the trash container, he became hostile. Yet Pam was no weakling. She carefully collected Mr. Frank's empties until she had a large grocery bag full of them, then she quietly took them to his office one night and dumped the whole mess on his desk over his papers, onto the floor, and into his chair.

You can picture the howls and outrage from her husband, but a good attorney knows when he is licked. That assertive episode on his wife's part cooled his belligerency and ended the embarrassing beer-can problem.

John Lambert, division superintendent for a multi-store paint and decorator's supply retailer, had a belligerent store manager who, for a year had refused to abide by the company's inventory guidelines. As a result, inventory turnover was poor, merchandise became obsolete, and store profits eroded. When John faced Jack Bulge, the store manager, he was again told to mind his own business and that Jack would run the store. To make matters worse, this was said in the hearing of store employees. Mr. Lambert forcefully replied: "Jack, either you agree to get and keep your inventory in line, or you are terminated as of today. You have exactly three seconds to make up your mind."

Jack made up his mind well within the prescribed time limit. With John Lambert's help, the inventory is now at acceptable levels, as is store manager Bulge's belligerent attitude.

Resolve, along with firm command action, can spare you needless embarrassment and frustration just as it did for Pamela Frank and John Lambert.

TIPS TO STOP THE TOUGH GUY COLD

The first control tip to remember in learning how to stop the tough guy cold is that nine times out of ten the disagreeable belligerent is not really all that tough. He is usually building up a tough facade in order to prove himself, and his self-concept is based solely on what others may think of him. This is not the way of self-power. PCP is based on your own inner convictions that you have the intellectual ability and determination to control the events and people around you. The belligerent does not have this inner confidence so his self-image is based on your reaction to his gross misconduct. If you succumb to his bully tactics, he will feel that he really is a tough, driving character. This will reinforce and encourage more wild, irrational behavior. But on the other hand, if you meet him with your own brand of command power, his ego will deflate and you will be able to assume full charge. This will benefit both you and your reluctant helper.

When you accept the premise that the boorish antagonist is not really as tough as he would like you to believe, you are then ready to apply specific techniques to stop him cold. These power tips will help you accomplish this.

1. Do not try to justify anything.

If you try to justify your position or prove it is the wiser one, you will fall into the trap the tough guy has already put *his* foot into. Don't bother for two reasons: one, the belligerent's mind is so closed that he won't accept what you say no matter how valid, and two, your opponent will misinterpret your motive. He will think your kind gesture indicates that he is controlling you, which will only lead to more fireworks. This will waste even more precious time because you will then have to clarify things for him.

2. Use the question technique.

You can deflate a belligerent with pointed questions that express your rejection of his childish antics. Such questions can also shock him into seeing the futility of continuing with the act he is putting on. The following questions will serve as models for you:

- You really don't like yourself, do you?
- Do you think you can intimidate me?

- You don't feel at all well, do you?
- Do you know that your face is getting red?
- Aren't you afraid of having a heart attack?
- Are you trying to scare me?
- Have you ever considered going on the stage?
- What in the world do you expect to gain by such behavior?
- Why are you acting like a forty-year-old teenager?
- What are you trying to prove?

Such questions challenge the belligerent because they show him that you see through his charade and are not very impressed. This will stop the tough guy cold, although he may still huff and puff a bit longer.

3. Ignore the culprit.

This is not always the easiest technique, but if you can manage it despite such flagrant belligerency, the tough guy will soon give up or at least change his tactics. This is because it's humiliating and discouraging for a belligerent to be ignored when he has a fight on his mind. Therefore, ignoring this character will frustrate and stop him if you choose this technique over the others. It probably won't be as much fun as using some other control techniques, but if it works for you that is good enough.

4. Show him that his opinion doesn't count.

Show the belligerent that his opposition is irrelevant to what you propose or are doing by showing him the facts and figures. If this solid line still doesn't stop the belligerent, state matter-of-factly that with or without him, you are going to accomplish what you have set out to do and if he wants to get in on the goodies, he will have to cooperate, and fast. And if not, he can give himself a nervous breakdown.

Norm Carr was the prime motivator of a group of four real estate brokers who made joint investments and later shared the profits. Mr. Carr had carefully surveyed a prize piece of property and had gotten the support of all members to buy at once, except for the objections of Stu Clayton who had bought into the group when Robert Gillian retired. Stu loudly and belligerently complained that interest rates were too high, that the property might be bought for less money by waiting, that the economy might falter, and that financing its sale might later be a problem, etc. Carr listened attentively, then advised Stu that he could talk until he was blue in the face, but the deal was going through with him or without him. His bluff called, Stu Clayton backed out of the deal, and six months later he jealously watched as his associates divided $120,000 profit.

What would have happened if Norm Carr had not stopped Stu Clayton cold? The deal would not have been consummated, the money would have gone to somebody else, and Mr. Clayton would still be resisting the aggressive businessmen who were supposed to be his associates.

Obviously, stopping the tough guy cold is a profitable exercise.

WHY BELLIGERENT CHARACTERS RESPECT COMMAND POWER

Belligerent characters respect command power because they see in it the essence of what they aspire to but have not been able to attain. This does not mean that every belligerent man or woman is a hopeless case. A more charitable explanation is that they have a somewhat confused and deficient outlook and suffer a serious psychological disorder for which you are not responsible. It also is not up to you to psychoanalyze them and try to correct the disability. You can, however, do them a favor by refusing to let them influence you with their destructive tactics. Your winning, despite their behavior, will show them the better way of asserting power and being a success. This is enough reason to apply command power in dealing with the tough guy, but the real payoff is that you get your way despite a misguided person's behavior. And, you even earn his respect in the process!

USE ACTION TO TEACH THE BELLIGERENT CHARACTER

Action is the only teacher the belligerent understands because it demonstrates your PCP and proves to the belligerent character that you will not be his victim. Emotionalism and well-intentioned words only encourage this tenacious opponent to keep his tactics up. But action closes the case and locks the door on your attacker.

Mike Bennett, a sales manager for Trenton Manufacturing and Supply, had realigned company sale territories for better coverage and more economical travelling. At the regular Monday morning sales meeting, he gave a detailed explanation of the changes and reasons for them, only to find that out of twenty-three sales people, *one* was violently opposed. This was F. B. Springer, a surly man who constantly had to be prodded to do his fair share of selling. After Mr. Springer jumped to his feet with a tirade labelling Mike as all wet, Mike unrolled a large map with the new territories clearly outlined. Looking squarely at Mr. Springer, he pointed to a territory, informed Mr. Springer that it was his new assignment, and explained that he was expected to make and keep it productive. With that, he announced that the subject was closed, and that the meeting would move on to the next subject on the agenda. And the matter *was* closed: Springer learned his lesson and is actually doing a good job with his new territory.

If you face a belligerent character who would like nothing better than to undermine your power, take action. Although he may have difficulty hearing what you say, your taking action will teach him that you mean business.

INSTANT POWER POINTERS

- Much belligerence is due to misunderstanding.
- To avoid being misunderstood:
    Don't pull your punches.
    Repeat—repeat—repeat!
    Highlight the benefits of cooperation.
    Don't apologize.

- Be prepared to meet an occasional belligerent.
- PCP will spare you frustration and embarrassment.
- To stop the tough guy cold:

  Do not try to justify anything.
  Use the question technique.
  Ignore the culprit.
  Show him that his opinion doesn't count.

- Belligerent characters respect command power.
- Action teaches the belligerent character that you mean business.

18

Power Secrets That Will Boost
Your Earning Ability

Big moneymakers have one thing in common: they know how to make effective use of people. This chapter will show you that getting things done through people is a prime secret in boosting your earning ability. And, as we have already seen, it is also a basic ingredient in developing more and more personal command power.

One final observation before we get into the specifics: people living in the Western hemisphere equate income with esteem. As a result, self-worth is often dependent upon financial status. While it is not the purpose of this chapter to debate the wisdom of that attitude, we must still recognize this hard fact which is not likely to change. This attitude exists throughout our society as is evidenced by the expression: "If you're so smart why aren't you rich?" Too, when evaluating a man, inevitably the question "What is he worth?" or "How much does he make?" is frequently heard.

The importance attached to earning ability somehow does not fit with the idea we are subtly taught as children, that it is "not nice" to talk about money. However, that is exactly what we are going to do now.

HOW TO MAP A POWER PLAN
TO ZOOM YOUR EARNING ABILITY

With the exception of a few rare geniuses, the really big moneymakers are adept at influencing and using others in order to attain their own financial goals. For this reason, your power plan for making more money must be based mostly on your ability to enlist and handle people. You can start using these next secrets today and get on your way to the money you want.

● **Pick people who are strong enough to help you earn more.**

It is comfortable to select helpers who are agreeable and easy to handle but it is also a trap. Instead, select your people on the basis of what they can do for you, because while it may stretch your command power to the limit to control some people in this group, that *is* what PCP is all about. Once you have decided how much money you want to earn, look around and find the people in a position to help you. Then, give these individuals your full attention.

Young Henry Bryan spent five years working under the nose of the president of a company which sold small engines and electrical components in a wide area. Henry had become financial vice-president, but there was no room for further advancement in that area. In addition, the company had a young president whose family insiders were lined up waiting for promotions within the firm's financial department. But young Bryan wanted more money and saw the opportunity to get it in the sales and marketing areas of the company. Here, only two men could help him get what he wanted: Tom Kelly, the aging vice-president of marketing, and R. A. Thompson, the company president. First, Henry bluntly asked Tom Kelly for a commitment to help move him into sales as Tom's assistant. Next, he went to R. A. Thompson and told him that he had a deal with Tom Kelly that needed Mr. Thompson's prompt approval. With some further maneuvering, Henry was the new assistant sales manager within thirty days, and with Tom Kelly's help, he was soon an expert. When Kelly retired a year later,

Henry became marketing vice-president, over the heads of older men in the department. Bryan is now earning substantially more in his new job than he could have hoped to have made had he not enlisted the aid of the two powerful men in his campaign to raise his earning level.

In picking people to help you earn more, start with the people nearest you. I used this tactic myself years ago, to move from accounting into sales promotion when I was working in the Fort Worth branch of a national concern. One day, Mr. Harry Rose, our southern supervisor, visited my branch. I took that opportunity to tell Mr. Rose that I had observed that the men behind desks were not making the substantial salaries in our company, and that I wanted in on sales where the action and money was. Further, I expressed a willingness to go where he needed me in order to make the change. Mr. Rose agreed that my observation was indeed accurate, and shortly thereafter, I was transferred to sales and earning more money. Within eighteen months, I was a young branch manager enjoying even more money. It frightens me to consider what would have happened had I chosen a less able helper than Mr. Rose: it might have taken me several years to cover the same ground.

Look at the people around you and pick the strongest ones you can find to be your best helpers in boosting your earning ability even more.

● **Demand what you deserve.**

You can use your command power to get paid what you are *worth*, which may be more than you are presently making.

First, let's assume that you have a job. If this is the case and you feel cheated because of a low pay scale, take some time to ask yourself what you are doing in that job. If the job has possibilities, or can lead to a better paying position, ask yourself what you can do to reach those higher income brackets. It may be worth staying with if you can eventually get the money you want. But beware of the out-dated idea that you are honor bound to stick with a job no matter what. Yes, you owe the job something, but the job owes you something too. If you get fired for demanding your dues, it isn't the end of the world: it could be the best thing that ever happened to you. As an individual with command power, there are plenty of opportunities open to you. And with that comforting thought, let's examine some techniques to get more money right where you are working.

First, be sure that you direct your strategy toward the right person. Remember, there is no point working with someone who has no authority to help you.

Once you have decided who can help you, do the unconventional: instead of asking for a raise for the traditional reasons, such as seniority or because you have learned that a fellow employee is making more, demonstrate exactly *why* you are worth more. This lays the groundwork for you to demand what you deserve.

John Clayton, a warehouse supervisor for a respected soft goods distributor, wanted more responsibility and the money that went with it. However, his company had a chronic problem being stuck with a number of slow-moving products that had to be sold at a loss. Seeing this as a golden opportunity, John worked up an inventory control portfolio showing the daily stock on hand, which items moved profitably, and which ones should be discontinued. Next, he took it to his company's president and insisted that he be allowed to try out his idea at once. Then when he finished detailing the advantages of his idea, John boldly stated that it should be worth more dollars to him as well as to the company. The president agreed, and the control system worked so well that John was promoted to buyer at a substantial salary increase.

When you back your demands for the earnings you deserve with facts and figures just as John did, your earning ability will skyrocket. When you know you are woth more, and you use command power to demonstrate it, you'll be soon on your way to big money.

Even if your job is untenable or the people in charge refuse to reward hard work and aggressiveness, there are options available. You don't even have to be someone's employee: there are many other ways to boost your earning power without working for someone else. You can become a self-employed entrepreneur and then nobody can tell you how much money you should make. The first step is to stop thinking that a job is the only way to get respect and money.

So, if you are in a dead end, no-money situation, make a list of the things you do well, assess the risks involved, and then become your own marketing expert. Some case histories of individuals who have gone out on their own and made it big will show you it's a chance worth taking.

Sandra Arbor worked for five years as the public relations director of a utility company. However, the salary she received was not commensurate with the demands made on her, and the board of directors turned a deaf ear to her each time she asked for a raise. Finally, Sandra gave notice and opened her own public relations firm, and ironically, at the end of the first year her old employer, the public utility, was among her clients paying her a fatter fee than the salary they had paid her at the utility as a full-time employee.

Jeff Burkland, an outdoorsman was also a frustrated, underpaid, high school coach. But as a hobby, Jeff made fishing lures and he was soon able to turn his hobby into a full-time job. He then became an employer himself, and boosted his earnings to three times his former salary!

Jan Sutherland, who worked as a cashier in a supermarket bakery, felt that she was underpaid and over-bossed. When Jan left the supermarket, she opened her own shop which specialized in wedding cakes and party favors. Today she even has a catering business, and she owes her satisfaction and greater earnings to her wise assessment of her career possibilities. She turned her command power loose, and capitalized on what she does best.

If you are stymied by a no-win job, consider *your* options. Make your choice and take the big step up to more cash, just as these determined moneymakers did.

● Assume responsibility for yourself.

When you commit yourself to making more money, you must be prepared to assume the responsibility for yourself. This means that once you have decided upon a plan, it becomes your responsibility to implement it. Therefore, when you make up your mind to boost your earning ability, the decision must be yours alone, and whatever happens next will also depend upon you. The risk is yours, but the rewards are also yours. And although it costs something to be a strong, self-responsible man or woman, it costs a great deal more to abdicate this responsibility which cannot be regarded frivolously. When you decide to live up to your responsibility to yourself in order to make more money, you must base your decision on sound reasoning. Here are the logical steps to be taken in this process:

1. Avoid an emotional decision.
2. Weigh the pros and cons.
3. Treat the decision as a business matter.
4. Make preliminary preparations.
5. Pinpoint your objectives.
6. Establish dollar goals.
7. Develop a time schedule.
8. Set down what you want to do in writing.
9. Don't over-shoot; be realistic.
10. Do not look back.

Let's make a brief assessment of each of these steps in order to emphasize the importance of arriving at a decision to earn more.

1. Avoid an emotional decision.

When a momentary decision is based on emotions, key factors bearing on the success of that decision are largely overlooked. Business decisions based on anger, frustration, revenge, hate, and rebellion are not power decisions. Avoid making monetary decisions when you are under stress or emotional strain because later, in the clear dawn of reason, these kinds of decisions all too often are wrong, or they are the right decisions at the wrong time, under the wrong circumstances. When you make a decision to increase your earning ability, use the cold logic of PCP to determine the time, the place, and the circumstances in which to do so. This way you can stay in control, and control is a key factor in boosting earning ability.

2. Weigh the pros and cons.

This step entails closely examining the advantages and dis-advantages of a project or plan to raise your income level. If the negative aspects outweigh the positive, you must then modify and strengthen your strategy. But if your idea has more positive aspects than negative ones, your chances of getting more money are favorable. All that is left to do in this case is to back your ideas up with action.

3. Treat the decision as a business matter.

Any decision regarding money is a no-nonsense business matter, so direct your financial improvement campaign on this basis. Marshall facts and figures to support your decision, and choose your helpers on the basis of their business power they can use in your behalf. As a result of going after more money as a business-minded professional, your vision will never be clouded by either emotion or pique.

4. Make preliminary preparation.

Self-responsibility demands careful preparation and plan-ning, because a decision to make more money should never be an impulsive, "fly-by-the-seat-of-the-pants" thing. Make pre-liminary preparations, but don't get bogged down in intricate details. Prepare to act, then go to it!

5. Pinpoint your objectives.

Don't aim for all the money in the world in one fell swoop. Instead, pinpoint your monetary objectives one at a time. You must also select helpers one at a time, since this way you will know where you are going and are able to leapfrog your earning ability from one peak to the next.

Reams have been written telling us that all we have to do is show people how to get what they want, and then they'll make you rich. It's great from an inspirational standpoint, since hav-ing others gain from your activities is a fringe benefit. However, your main objective is to increase your earning ability, so be sure to pinpoint *that* in your mind while you establish your financial objectives.

6. Establish dollar goals.

When you decide to improve your earning ability, give meaning to it by establishing actual dollar goals. Decide how much money you want to make tomorrow or next year, and give it a dollar sign, i.e., $1000, $10,000, or $100,000. Make it concrete by using a dollar sign: this will encourage you to do your best, and it will also serve as a guideline for your progress up the ladder to financial reward.

7. Develop a time schedule.

Deciding *when* you want to earn more is as important as deciding how you want to earn it. Setting a time limit for yourself will also discourage dilly-dallying, indecision, and rationalizing. So, circle a date on your calendar, and go!

8. Set down what you want in writing.

When you put something on paper, you also engrave it in your mind. It doesn't matter how good your memory is, or how keen your determination; nothing takes the place of writing down what you want because a written commitment keeps you on track. It will serve as a constant reminder that you have a responsibility to yourself.

9. Don't over-shoot.

In mapping a strategy to fulfill your responsibility to yourself and to boost your earning capacity, don't over-shoot. Rather, be realistic, and go after what you can reasonably hope to get. Then, as your earning skills grow, you can earn more and more. Remember that an unrealistic first goal can lead to discouragement and depression, while a realistic goal can build confidence, develop skills, and lead to higher goals.

Don't forget: writing it down keeps you from going after too little as well as too much.

10. Don't look back.

Once you have embarked on a program to boost your earning capacity, don't look back. There will be nothing gained from worrying about something already behind you, so don't look back. All that is behind you is less money than you wanted—then or now.

HOW TO MAKE THE BOSS NOTICE YOU

It is a fact of the times that there are far more employees than there are people who are self-employed. It follows then, that there are also more people who must get the attention of their bosses first before their earning ability can skyrocket. Try these suggestions to get the attention you'll need:

- **Ask for more responsibility.**

The employee who is brash enough and honest enough to tell the boss that he wants more responsibility will get the bosses' attention. In an atmosphere where most employees eschew responsibility, it is always a pleasant surprise when someone walks in and tells the boss he wants more. Don't waste your command power by only asking for more responsibility; strengthen your request by explaining that you want the extra money that goes with it. Your boss can respect that, and after one such approach, he or she will be watching you closely. This is because when you are strong enough to ask for more responsibility and money, you demonstrate your drive and power. As you prove yourself, your employer will find even more responsibility for you. Don't hesitate to demand the money that goes with the added duties.

- **Do more than you were hired to do.**

Does this sound old-fashioned? It still is a most effective way to get the boss to notice you. The difference between yesterday and today, though, is that the boss will wonder what is wrong with you if you don't ask for more money on the basis of your unusual performance.

- **Bring the boss an idea.**

Ideas are priceless assets that will boost your earning capacity. And, bosses prize ideas: they notice them and the creative people who generate them, so take your boss an idea on cost-cutting, saving money, sales techniques, office efficiency, or anything else that will improve employee performance. If he doesn't show his appreciation in a tangible way, go in and tell him that you would like to keep contributing ideas while on the job, but that the name of the game is money. Be careful to phrase the demand to suit your personality and the occasion because the boss is no dummy. He will soon get the idea.

● Tell the boss you are worth more, and tell him why.

Never hesitate to tell the boss you are worth more if you feel that you deserve more. But be sure to tell him why. It is not enough to wait until you are angry and disgusted to go in and explode, complaining that you are worth more. You can be reasonable and forceful while making a firm statement of fact; this is also much more effective. The following will give you a picture of the tack to use.

> If you are in sales, show the boss your sales figures. And don't forget to show him how you plan to produce even more.
>
> If you are in production, show your production level and time records. Tell him or her how you plan to improve those figures, too.
>
> If you are in an office, explain how you have assumed more and more of the workload; then ask for even greater responsibilities.

When you present your case, have the fixed dollar amount you expect in mind. Tell the boss that it is what you want, now. Then he will know that you will be back when you are ready for more money. The point here is to use your power to insure that you are paid for what you do. The boss will know that you won't expect more and you should not accept less. This will keep your earning ability moving.

One last note on getting the boss to notice you: don't become a pest. Employees who send the boss a steady stream of memos or pop in and out of his office like a grasshopper will be looked upon as a pest. The salary of a pest does not soar. When you want more money, build yourself a strong case along the lines we have discussed, and present it along with the dollar amount you want. Do this as if you expect nothing less than full agreement and the boss will notice your aggressiveness and determination. If this doesn't work, go back and read the earlier observations on your options. There is more than one way a person using command power can boost his earning ability.

HOW A MIDWEST SALESMAN WENT FROM $12,000 A YEAR TO $70,000 A YEAR

Andrew Skiffington, an ambitious salesman with his sights on big money, was earning $12,000 annually selling oil field and drilling supplies. His volume justified a much healthier salary, but when Andy went to his boss and asked to be put on straight commission or a salary plus bonus arrangement, he was coldly rebuffed. Two weeks later Andy quit and went out on his own as a manufacturer's rep. As his former employer's competitor, he went from $12,000 a year to $70,000 in just twelve short months. As Mike Grovernor, Andy's former boss, ruefully remarked, it cost him a lot more to lose a determined salesman than Andy's proposed deal would have. As for Andy, he is not mad at anybody: he's too busy boosting his already hefty earning ability.

As Andy's case exemplifies, whether you stay where you are or strike out in a new direction, you owe it to yourself to keep your earning ability in high gear. That power option is yours.

HOW TO DEAL WITH ENVY AND JEALOUSY AS YOUR MONEY POWER GROWS

Every command power personality with exciting earning ability must invariably face a few disgruntled associates and acquaintances. These problem people are afflicted with unreasonable envy and jealousy which is as old as time. But they must be dealt with constructively and the following secrets will show you how to handle the problem.

- **Ignore the problem:**

If you have reason to believe that an envious individual is going to cool it after a little burst of self-pity and jealousy, then you can ignore him. Anything as petty as envy and jealousy deserves to be ignored unless the misguided individual is bent on causing you discomfort or trouble. In that case, you must deal with your sick opponent promptly and directly by trying this:

- **Deal with it on a one-on-one basis.**

When an envious person becomes unbearable by publicly smearing you, call him aside. Deal with him privately, face to face, and demand that he cease his childish behavior. Explain that he is making a fool of himself and convincing no one. Belittle his attitude and conduct, demand a firm commitment to retract his statements, and extract an agreement from him that his attitude and conduct will be altered at once. If he is totally unresponsive, remind him that there are legal remedies for libel in the courts, but use this threat only when all else has failed. Then, back up your threat.

- **Tell 'em there is more room at the top.**

Strong individuals do not use their command power to commit mayhem unless they are allowed no other choice. The same sense and judgment that makes them strong and productive in the first place dictates that they deal with annoying and petty jealousy in a constructive way. I'm sure you will agree that it is far better to get the unfortunate, envious opponent on a positive track than to succumb to the urge to knock his teeth out. You can help him or her by pointing out that there is always room at the top for those willing to pay the price. Use your own experience in achieving a better income to point the way for this unhappy, confused individual. In the process, it is entirely possible that you can make a useful ally of him, which is far better than keeping up a running dogfight or totally destroying some weak, envious personality. Be big-hearted any time and any place you can, but with this one restrictive clause: remain in charge of your own financial goals. This is the heart of all power secrets that boost your earning ability.

INSTANT POWER POINTERS

- Big moneymakers use people effectively.
- Feeling self-worth often depends upon financial status.
- In mapping a power plan to boost your earning ability:

  > Pick strong helpers
  > Demand the rewards you deserve
  > Assume responsibility for yourself
  > Make no emotional decisions
  > Establish dollar goals
  > Set time limits

- Make the boss notice you.
- You have several moneymaking options.
- You owe it to yourself to keep your earning ability in high gear.
- Every power figure with exciting earning ability will face some disgruntled, envious people.
- Remain in charge of your own financial goals.

19

How to Give Your Command Power a Boost with Time Control

Everybody, from the cabbie to the President of the United States, has exactly twenty-four hours in a day. Yet some people never seem to have enough time to keep up with their daily routines, while others use the same amount of time to manage their lives and their fortunes effectively. The difference is this: some people use their personal power to manage their time while others drift along with time and tide. Some people always feel that they have more to do than they have time for, while stronger personalities keep ahead of their routine and make the time to eagerly entertain new ideas and develop new goals. The secret is that these are the ones who give their command power a boost by using time control. In this chapter you will find the observations, secrets, and techniques that can put you in the same time zone as these winners.

NEVER SAY "I DON'T HAVE TIME"

Never say "I don't have time." It is a deceptive expression that brainwashes you and becomes a power-crippling crutch.

What you really mean when you say "I don't have time" is one of two things:

1: "I'm disorganized, indecisive, confused, and have lost control."

2: "I have priorities, and have chosen to do something else that has more meaning and profit for me. I'm in charge, and I have decided to spend my time on something other than what you suggest."

If you are in the #2 category, you have already developed power strategies that boost your command power. You are controlling your time, and are using this priceless commodity as it is meant to be used: to get things done and to get what you want. If you are struggling along in area #1, these next techniques and experiences can put you on the right track. For those of you in the #2 category, this material will give you extra firepower.

First, consider the two main aspects of time.

A. Hours

Hours are used to measure time, and are the unit we employ to divide the day into manageable parts. They are a control scale that tells us whether we are productively using the day as it progresses, or whether we are apathetically and indifferently letting it slip by. Hours are important, and they are always the same: they give one man no more than they do the next. Therefore, they are yours to treasure or squander. Only you can make the choice.

B. Power

The second aspect of time is power. Power involves what you do with the hours in each day. When you squander, waste, misuse, or ignore these hours, you weaken your command power. Each neglected hour gives your opponent that much more advantage because time is a silent partner. It marches beside you with a steady beat and is there to do your bidding, so control it, use it. It is a real power component.

TIME CONTROL:
A MATTER OF PRIORITIES

Time is a matter of priorities because you cannot do every-thing at the same time and you cannot be all things to all people every hour. If you are to use time as the power tool that it can be, then you must control that tool. Do this by establishing priori-ties: decide what you will do each day, break the day into hours, assign each hour its priorities, and then stick to them. This will give every day a full measure of power. Note how the people in these case studies; busy, power-conscious people, utilize time to control and direct their personal power.

Ned Pipkin was once a harried over-worked executive. Before he got his priorities in order, he would buy the morning paper on the way to work. As he walked to his office, he would pass Ed Gomes, the sports fan's desk and every day they went into a fifteen-minute ritual rehashing of the previous night's game. Then, another twenty minutes or so was spent thumbing through the paper. At about this time, his secretary would bring in a cup of coffee and the unopened morning mail, and drinking the coffee and opening and sorting the mail would occupy another thirty minutes. Next, a few social calls from cronies and/or his wife took another half-hour, in addition to the other petty interruptions which would waste another thirty minutes or so. The afternoons were not much better.

Ned says that late one evening about midnight, as he sat looking at a pile of work he had brought home, he saw the light. Half of his day was out of control! He decided then and there to act like the power figure that he was paid to be. So he stopped reading the paper in his office, merely said "Good morning" to Ed and moved along, had his secretary open and distribute the mail, and set up a definite time limit for taking phone calls or greeting visitors. He then earmarked the time gained to set up appointments, schedule meetings, make decisions, and other-wise do his work. Now, his daily business routine runs smoothly and efficiently, and he no longer needs to burn the midnight oil trying to recapture the time frittered away during the day. He is in charge.

Mary Beecher, a working mother and housewife, was chronically late in getting to her office. The reasons? Her friends called her in the early morning to catch her at home, her two children were assigned no chores, and her husband spent hours staring at the boob tube. Mary easily turned the situation around by simply refusing to answer the phone before going to work, assigning each child responsibilities, and turning off her husband's TV until household chores were shared and finished. Now that her priorities are in order, Mary arrives at the office refreshed and on time.

Tim Potts was a real estate agent who was always busier than the proverbial cranberry merchant, yet his contemporaries always managed to see more prospects and sell more houses than he. Tim agonized over this situation until he discovered his trouble. He was actually taking people out for a lot of expensive joy rides because he did not qualify his prospects first. Now Tim began qualifying each prospect and refusing to waste his days chauffeuring a lot of losers around. His new priority was to spend every hour selling. This not only saved him precious time, but it also boosted his sales ratio. He even ended up as salesman of the year!

HOW TO MAKE TIME

Your power grows in relation to the way you control your time. The more time you make for yourself, the more you will be in a position to wheel and deal your personal command power. Conversely, if you fritter your time away or let it slip between your fingers like sand, you will be wasting your power trying to keep up with simple daily routines. These concrete methods and examples will help you make and control your time.

Of course, making time is a figure of speech. Nobody literally makes more time, and as we have noted, there is the same amount for yesterday, today, and tomorrow. Making time really means pushing aside the time traps that can clutter your day; it means putting your mind, your power, and your energy into getting or accomplishing what is most important to you. Thus, you control and manage your time. You can make more time for the important things by delegating lesser projects to one of your helpers, or by refusing to be side-tracked by unimportant details.

Steps to use in controlling and making time:

1. Decide what you expect from your time.
2. Make a written day by day plan delineating what you want from each hour.
3. Apply your time where it will get you the most.
4. Use your people power to delegate jobs and projects.
5. Give full attention to the job you are doing.
6. Make your helpers time conscious.
7. Respect the dollar value of each hour.
8. Learn how to use time without being a slave to the clock.

Item 1.

Basically, your concern is to get the most out of each working day. You need to manage your time so that you won't have to spend all your working hours chasing the details thrust upon you. You must take some time in which you can be creative, develop ideas, and plan where to use your aggressive power for maximum impact. You must decide what you actually expect from your time.

Here are some effective decision-making steps to help you get what you want and expect of your time.

A. Get routine matters out of the way early in the day.
B. Decide what else you want to accomplish that day.
C. See only those people who can help you reach your goal for the day.
D. Discipline yourself to finish what you have planned for the day.

Item 2.

The best way to attain your goals and expectations of your time is to make a daily, written plan. Don't just list a lot of "must do" items each day, but instead list things in order of importance and then assign each project its own particular time slot. Treat each item as a plane you have to catch at the particular time you have allotted to it: nobody dilly-dallies if he has to get on a plane in order to accomplish something important. Regard your daily timetable in this way, and with the same intense discipline you would use to get to the airport on time.

Item 3.

Put in your time where it will accomplish what you want. To determine if you are really doing this, for one week keep a diary of everything you do each day. You may be surprised at how much time you can save for yourself by cutting out the many activities that add nothing to your day or your command power. The following are examples compiled by a sales executive who kept just such a time diary of thoughtless activities which he promptly eliminated.

- Making too many calls for his salesmen instead of training them to handle the tough accounts on their own.
- Spending too much time on expense accounts which were always well within limits anyway.
- Making calls his secretary could make.
- Opening and reading every circular, advertisement, and trade item that crossed his desk.
- Making too many speeches in too many places that had nothing to do with his own goals and objectives.
- Accepting luncheon dates with people who bore him.
- Taking all phone calls, no matter how trivial.
- Waiting until the last minute to decide on monthly promotions.
- Holding too many needless sales meetings.
- Interviewing all applicants regardless of their potential.
- Drinking too much coffee.
- Playing golf during working hours.
- Rationalizing that *all* sales managers had more to do than they could handle.

Virgil Newport, the sales executive who kept this revealing diary, added one full day to his workweek by eliminating these time-stealing activities. Not only was his own effectiveness enhanced when he began using his time on priority goals, but his whole sales force also picked up some of his renewed power and enthusiasm.

Item 4.

Use your people power to delegate jobs and projects because this is a way of using your command power. Obviously, the more you can delegate responsibility, the more time you will make for yourself. One key factor to consider in delegating your authority and responsibility: make certain that they understand what is to be done in your behalf. Otherwise, you may have to waste valuable time in doing it over. It is vital that you hand over activities to others with clear instructions.

Item 5.

When you give full attention to the job you are doing right now, you are controlling your time. This is tantamount to making or adding time because every distraction or interruption wastes valuable minutes. Rivet your attention and your power on a particular job: it will save time and help get you what you want.

Item 6.

Make your helpers time conscious, otherwise your programs, projects, and goals will straggle along haphazardly, with little regard for what you need, or when you need it. When delegating projects, assigning authority, and motivating people to move in your behalf, set the time limits and explain them forcefully and clearly in your instructions. A meeting of minds right from the start will put you in charge of your time, and it will also make your helpers time conscious.

Item 7.

You've heard the old adage that time is money. You can believe it. Respect the dollar value of each hour; this way you will get a picture of what your time is worth monetarily. To arrive at the dollar value of an hour, divide the money you make by the hours it took to make it. The answer, the quotient, gives you a dollars-and-cents reason to boost your command power by using time control.

Item 8.

You can use time to boost your power without becoming a slave to the clock. When you use the ideas and techniques explained in items one through seven you can avoid this and still increase your power. The point is in using your time to get what you want, by influencing others to help you do just that. Make time serve you: employ the time control techniques in this chapter and you will never be a slave to the clock. Instead, you will be its master.

HOW TO BOOST YOUR POWER WITH TIME-MAKING SPEECH

Every time you open your mouth to direct or motivate someone, you are, in effect, making a speech. Time is also an element of speech; it can create extra time for you, or it can waste it for you and whoever you work with. These two helpful hints will show you how you can boost your command power with time-making speech:

● **Focus your speech like a hypodermic needle.**

By the time you are ready to direct and control someone, you must make clear what you want him or her to do for you. Be specific, because unless you tell your helper exactly what you want him to do, he may do one thing while you may have an entirely different project in mind. For example, the president of a retail chain once had an unprofitable store that he felt could be made highly profitable. So he called in his assistant and said, "Our Hillsford store is losing money. Go out and put a stop to it within one month!" At the end of the month, the young assistant proudly reported, "I sold the Hillsford store, all right." Much time and money was thereby lost due to faulty communication on the president's part.

How could the president have focused his speech with time-making power? These examples explain it:

"Go out and put that store on its feet within one month."

"Go out and turn that store around!"

"Go out and correct the problem!"

Your helpers can't do what you want until they understand what it is. To protect your time, be specific and focus your directions completely.

● **Make your speech exciting.**

When your speech excites your helpers, you will build extra time and power for yourself. This is because people get excited when they expect something good to happen to them. Therefore, excite your helpers with dramatic words that show them how they will benefit by cooperating with you. One sales supervisor for a direct sales company put large colorful photos of two houses on the wall. One was a picture of an elegant house in the best part of town, while the other was a modest home in need of a paint job. When his group assembled for the next week's regular sales meeting, he pointed to the lavish house and said, "When you do as I say, you can live in a home like this." This simple, direct speech, augmented by a picture of what they could get, excited the audience to action. Obviously, sales moved.

You will make extra time and boost your power when you focus your speech and make it exciting for your helpers. Be sure to plan it that way.

HOW TO CONTROL SOCIAL TIME

In and out of the business world, a great deal of time is lost to too much socializing by people who are bored to tears. Although it is not necessary, we want to be known as nice, agreeable people. So we become trapped, lose control, and time flies out the window. The harried business executive gives up precious time to see a casual visitor who is supposed to be an old buddy. The housewife with an outside job lets Mary, Jane, Alice, and Elizabeth gab to her on the phone about nothing important. The salesman lingers over a too-long lunch with a talkative crony and winds up late for an important appointment. They all feel obliged to be sweet and sociable, even though they are bored stiff. But, nobody is under obligation to waste time on uninvited or unexpected social intrusions, so don't be a victim of the social intruder.

How do you control your time rather than sacrificing it to unwanted social intrusions along with your power? Try the following ideas:

First, weigh the consequences. Ask yourself what the worst thing that can happen to you is if you refuse to be trapped into wasting time on thoughtless intruders? At the worst, you might hear a few baseless expressions of surprise and affected outrage. On the other hand, when you refuse to be a social victim, you will stay in control of your time. Your power and self-confidence will have received a satisfying boost.

Let's look at how the three victims we described might have given their command power a needed boost using firm time control.

In the case of the business executive, he should have his secretary screen visitors and protect him from casual drop-ins. Or, he could quickly explain to his visitor that he has a full schedule and would have to see him at a more convenient time. Another option would be to have his secretary obtain the drop-in's phone number, with the executive's promise to call him.

The housewife/career woman has a number of options: she can have other family members answer the phone and explain that she is busy and cannot talk at the moment. Or, if she chooses to answer the phone herself, she can tell the caller that she cannot talk now and then promptly hang up. Too, she can advise her social callers that she will take calls only at a given time of her own choosing.

The salesman's utter disregard for time is not defensible. He should tell his persistent crony that he has an appointment, and then go.

You do not have to rule out all social activities. On the contrary, you *should* participate in them because you owe it to yourself and to your friends. The point is: social time, like all time, *must* be controlled by you. The friends who count will understand.

HOW TO GET THE MOST FROM OTHER PEOPLE'S TIME

When you motivate and control people, you are using their time. How much you influence them to do for you will depend on how well you direct and control their time. These steps will insure that you get the most from your helpers' time.

1. Assign definite projects.
2. Establish specific time schedules.
3. Make progress checks.
4. Compare progress with time allotted.

Specific projects must be assigned to insure that you'll get the most from other people's time. This is why sales and production quotas are established, and why time and motion studies are made. When you decide who to use, you are careful to select only helpers that you know have enough of their own power to help you. If you use the same care in assigning projects, goals, and duties, if you are explicit, you will boost your power while getting the most from your helpers' time.

You must establish exact time schedules in order to extract the most from other people's time. For example, what purpose would it serve for a sales manager to assign quotas, and then fail to establish a specific time for them to be met? Production quotas would also mean nothing unless they were to be filled within a time limit. *When* your helpers finish your assignment, is as important as *what* they do.

To control the time of those you direct, make progress checks at regular intervals. These will remind your helpers that they are expected to perform on time, and will also identify any laggards so that you can get them back on schedule without a great time-loss.

Progress checks are useless to you unless you lay them side

by side with what has been accomplished: when you compare progress with the time allotted to complete a project, you will know at once how your helpers are performing. This puts you in a position to take corrective measures if necessary and, in any event, as the person in charge, you will be keeping an accurate record of how effectively you manage your peoples' time. When you've compared the progress made with the time you have allotted, you will have this time control information.

TIME: THE MOST VALUABLE POWER ASSET YOU HAVE

Time is the most valuable power asset you will ever have, and it takes a strong command personality to face the fact that the amount you have is limited. Unfortunately, most people live and work as if forever were their middle name; but nobody lives forever. Command power is for *now*, the time that you have is *now*, so give your personal command power a boost with your exclusive power asset: time.

INSTANT POWER POINTERS

- Everybody has 24 hours in a day.
- Never say "I don't have time."
- Time has two notable divisions: hours and power.
- Time control is a matter of priorities.
- You can make and control time by:

> Deciding what you expect from time.
> Making a written day-by-day plan.
> Applying time where it will get you what you want.
> By delegating jobs and projects.
> By giving full attention to the job you are doing.
> Making your helpers time-conscious.
> Respecting the dollar value of every hour.
> Mastering the clock.

- Boost your power with time-making speech.
- Control social time by controlling intruders.
- Get the most from other people's time.
- Time is the most important power asset you have.

20

Strategies and Emphasis to Keep Your Personal Command Power Red Hot

Who has the most to lose if you neglect your personal command power? Who has the most to gain when you forcefully apply your PCP on a day-to-day basis? Obviously, you do. Now that you have the techniques, the methods, and the systems to make the most of your power, here are key strategies to keep your command power red hot. Use this strategy line-up as a ready reference, and be sure to review it from time to time: they will insure that you are regularly employing each and all of the components of your personal power effectively and constructively in going after what you want.

1. ZERO IN ON WHAT IS IMPORTANT TO YOU

There are two vital steps in zeroing in on what you want. They are, 1, deciding what is important to you and, 2, hanging in until you get it.

PCP gives you a great deal, but it also demands much, such as firm, clean, sharp decisions. The first step in focusing your power is to choose the target. However, before you zero in on what you want, you must decide what is important to you. Once this is done—and not a minute before—you can map your strategies to get what you want.

Deciding what you want is a personal matter, and a decision for *you* to make and implement. You cannot afford to let someone else decide what is important for you, or what you want. If you are being victimized by someone who is deciding what is best for you, you will be handicapped in obtaining your goals. Rather than devoting all your energy and power to single-mindedly pursuing your goal, you will instead be dealing with resentment, self-recrimination, and frustration. Therefore, make your own power decisions and let the end results be yours: there has never been a "no-charge" advisor who did not want to share the glory and the goodies if his advice proved helpful, nor has there ever been one who was willing to share in the pain of failure if his advice proved disastrous and heartbreaking.

Hanging in (perseverance) demands certain qualities and power. Since you have the power, let's touch on the necessary qualities involved. View your goals and objectives as your responsibility, and follow your own rules. When the opposition shows its fangs, don't become upset, emotional, or discouraged. Don't waste time vacillating whether to back up or delay your project. Rather, use the qualities described above and you will get results.

Harry T. Silsby had decided to borrow $900,000 to double his warehouse space, but his accountant squawked that this wasn't feasible because his business was less than two years old. But Harry persisted: he took his financial statement and a resumé of his new company to his banker, and sure enough, he was turned down. Harry suffered two more rebuffs, but then the largest bank in town granted him the loan. Harry's warehouse space doubled, business expanded, and the loan was promptly repaid. Harry's new banker muses that it was Harry's perseverance and spirit more than his financial statement that led to his approving the loan.

It has been said that with ordinary talent and extraordinary perseverance, all things are attainable. Add your own brand of personal power to that and you have an unbeatable combination.

2. KEEP YOUR EYE ON THE WINNERS

Jake McCurdy, a retired millionaire salesman, when asked how he had attained such heights with only an eighth-grade education, always answered, "I watched the winners." Jake not only watched the winners, he cultivated their friendship and learned their secrets.

Keeping an eye on the winners is an excellent strategy to keep your power hot. When you see your contemporaries doing the things you want to do and obtaining things you would like to have, then you realize that you are not whistling in the dark. Pick up their techniques and add them to your own: this will give you an extra advantage that even the winners you admire haven't got.

Lee Hammons was a sensitive young man trying to make it on the road as a novice salesman. His volume of business was growing, but handling irascible customers shot his nerves and left him discouraged. Then one day he watched a one hundred and thirty-five pound salesman work over a tough machine shop owner. Lew Foster, the machine shop proprietor, was berating his salesman, John McClean, because it had taken four weeks to get delivery on some equipment he had ordered, and he threatened never to order from him again. Mr. McClean then said, "Lew, that might not be a bad idea if you can't believe or remember what I say. Pull your order copy: you will see that I noted that the delivery would take four or five weeks. You are too smart to be making threats, especially when you don't know what you are talking about. Check it out so we can quit wasting time and get back to business." Foster hesitated, grumbled that it wouldn't be necessary, then benignly gave Mr. McClean another order.

What Lee learned from this observation was that he had been acting apologetically and was embarrassed whenever a belligerent customer laid into him. It doesn't happen now, however. What Lee learned from watching a winner gave him the added incentive to get what he wanted despite anyone's blustery tactics.

Jim Wilson, whose terrifying weakness was speaking, watched a high-powered businessman in action. After hearing Mr. Trotter present an after-dinner talk to a group of community leaders, Jim hesitantly asked him his secret. Mr. Trotter was pleased, and invited Jim to join his civic club where they could work together. Soon Jim had audiences watching him make winning speeches and demonstrations.

Charles Hillhouse, a top-flight realtor, always instructs new salespeople to keep an eye on the company's winners, and the strategy works. Hillhouse has more million-dollar salesmen than his two closest competitors.

Keep your eye on the winners, but don't watch them for the excitement only. Watch them to pick up and adopt extra power secrets: they will be flattered, and your power will be sizzling.

3. DON'T BE DONE IN BY FEAR OF FAILURE

No matter how well you plan, no matter how carefully you weigh the odds, there is no guarantee that you will always succeed. But this is not the key factor in keeping your power hot. Rather, you must be willing to take the risk, and to use your power forcefully. Then, if you run into an impossible situation, it is important not to panic. Simply accept an unavoidable setback as nothing more than a temporary delay, regroup, and then go after what you want using a different approach. Don't let yourself be done in by fear of failure.

At this point in your power-training, it is highly unlikely that fear of failure is overwhelming you. If fear of failure is a problem for you, go back and review chapter thirteen. When you heat up your command power, this fear will fade, as does fear in any form when action walks through the door.

4. BE WILLING TO PAY THE PRICE

Paying the price for a red-hot PCP does not suggest that the price is prohibitive. Instead, consider the price of neglecting PCP; this is the destructive figure. The price you must be willing to pay in order to keep your power hot is more constructive than costly, and it consists of:

Desire
Determination
Observation
Study
Preparation
Action

Power means nothing unless there is the desire to use it, heat it up, and put it to work. Desire is not something that can be handed to you in a bucket: it springs from within you; it is something you must give yourself; it is akin to ambition and attitude, and it is part of the price of a hot command power.

Determination is the grit that converts desire into reality. It is the power or habit of deciding, definitely and firmly. It is a price you must be willing to pay for effective personal power, but it is not too steep a cost: rather, it is an asset of the first magnitude, and is the torch of character and spirit.

When you make a habit of deciding, definitely and firmly, what you want and how you will get it, the result will be PCP hot enough to get the job done.

Observation is the ability to recognize and analyze what goes on about you, and entails the capacity to make valid judgments and decisions based on what you have observed. You observe when you watch the winners and losers; doing so enables you to separate fact from fiction. And since it gives you a base from which to rocket your command power, when you pay the price of observation as part of the cost of a red hot command power, the dividends will be yours to keep.

Studying is a small price to pay for anything: it keeps your power current, up-to-date, and glowing, it never finds a comfortable little plateau to rest in, it enables you to cope with change, keep up with trends, markets, demography, psychological advances, techniques and the methods that constantly bear on PCP. I recommend it highly.

I know of strong leaders, well into their sixties, who make

room for college courses in their still busy schedules. This participation in formal study insures that their power will not get stuck in a rut of out-dated ideas and moldy opinions. These vibrant, productive people also read widely. Their studies expose them to new ideas, techniques, and dynamic contemporary power concepts, just as it will for you.

Studying is another price you shouldn't be concerned with paying, because it lights a fire within you that returns money, power, and satisfaction, over and over again. Studying is an expansive (as opposed to expensive) strategy that will give fire and direction to your PCP.

● Preparation

There are many facets to preparation, such as observation and studying. In terms of command power, preparation is the mapping of strategies and otherwise equipping yourself to nail down goal after goal. PCP does not zig-zag like a random flash of lightning across a turbulent sky: if you pay the price, you will hit your targets. The better you prepare, the hotter your command power will become.

● Action

Action is the prime secret in keeping your PCP hot and putting your power to work. It cannot be emphasized too much, because dreams, plans, aspirations, observation, studying, and preparation all mean nothing until you act. The first name of the power game is *action*.

The price of inaction is awesome: depression, loss of power, loss of friends, loss of respect and whatever else is of consequence to you. Inaction thrives on excuses and self-pity, so, in view of this, let's get on to your basic concern: action that generates power.

There are two major considerations in the launching of power action: one, establishing a course of action and, two, selecting the best time to begin it. The following example illustrates the point.

(1) If you were going to sell a fleet operator six new, over-the-road rigs, you would gather all the relative information and

figures, rehearse your presentation, and make sure you have a good load of ammunition with which to do the job.

(2) You would not go in with the drivers on strike or 50% of the fleet idle, but rather when the rigs were on the road, the drivers working, and the customer doing business.

A sales manager for a top wholesale distributor says, "I don't look for the brightest men when I employ a new man. I look for one that wants to go." His record lends credence to his philosophy.

The price of action can be exacting; the price of inaction cannot be computed. One thing is certain: pay the price of action and you will keep your power red hot. And that is worth money and much more.

5. CONTROL YOUR POWER ATTITUDE

An attitude, as it applies to your personal command power, is a feeling or emotion about your power. Your power attitude is your mental fix or position toward what you can and cannot do. Like all abstract personality qualities, your attitude is yours and yours alone. You must control it or else it will control you. When you control your attitude, you are a decision-making action-minded power figure.

Consider this thought in regard to your power attitude: be your own built-in consultant. Yes, talk to others if you wish. Weigh their counsel, but make the power decisions on your own, because it is what *you* think that matters, not what they think, and what *you* want that counts, not what they want.

When you control your power attitude, you control your self-image. If you see yourself as a power-loaded man or woman, you will work and win on that basis. It is sweet to have the flattery and regard of others, but what you accomplish and the way you use your power is the bottom line. When you control your attitude to set your power on fire, you are your own hero. And that is as it should be.

6. KICK POWER-ROBBING HABITS

Habit is a repetitious attitude or action which requires no thinking. Power-robbing habits attach themselves like leeches to their victim, yet, strange as it sounds, these destructive, thieving habits can become dear to their victims, and mental habits are the hardest of all to kick. These obscure reason, cloak themselves in excuses, and boot power out the window. Nevertheless, pernicious habits can be licked if you use the following plan.

Make a list of habits which you may subconsciously tolerate or use as convenient excuses. This list might include such habits as:

- Comparing yourself to others.
- Seeking reassurances from associates.
- Punishing yourself with "what ifs."
- Waiting until the "right" time.

There are numerous other annoying habits, but these are high among the power-robbers. Too, these four serve as examples of similar habits that are equally damaging. Once you have taken the all-important step of isolating and identifying a robbing-habit, get rid of it by refusing to become a victim of yourself. Substitute healthier attitudes and habits for the insidious thieving ones. For example:

- Do not compare yourself to anyone else because this is a false scale. You are you: your power is yours, so use it to get what you want. You do not need an outside model. If you concentrate on you, it will keep you out of the comparison trap.
- If you explore a power project by the devious route of seeking assurances from associates and friends, you will develop a habit that wastes time and means nothing, because friends and associates will pat you on the back just to get you out of their hair. They can afford to lay on the little assurances; after all, what do they have to lose? As we have noted, you must be your own consultant. This will insure that your PCP keeps hot, since it will be based on logic and perception rather than flippancy or the tranquilizing opinion of friends and associates.
- Punishing yourself by habitually exploring and entertaining every "what if," will not only slow down power; it will also render it useless. Of course, there are risks involved in

boldly putting power to work, but the remedy that knocks the uncomfortable and debilitating habit of agonizing over "what if" is to use your skill, techniques, and available facts by stacking them against the "what ifs." This comparison will give you reason to apply the fire to your power.

Another thought to eliminate this power-robbing habit is: "What if" you never used your power at all?

There can be more than one right time to do something, but there will never be an ideal time, and there are *no* ideal people, any time, anywhere. Remember that power is a people tool, so do not get into the habit of waiting for the right time to motivate, control, use, employ, and inspire people; do not wait for the ideal time to light the fire of your PCP. If you wait, the flame will die in your hands and your power will turn to ashes.

● One personally gratifying way to keep your power red hot is to put your critics in the back row. Obviously, you will never get rid of these self-righteous, insecure noise-makers, but you can keep them in place, which is in the back row where they can criticize to their hearts content without detracting from either your power or your power plans in any way.

Critics have an inborn tendency to ignore facts. Their specialty is opinion: theirs. This one-man opinion is nothing more than that—one man's opinion. It may have absolutely no bearing on what you want, what you can do, or what your goals are, and certainly not on the power you choose to exercise. Critics who sit on the sidelines, like parrots on a perch, have a great capacity for looking at the facts and then reaching the wrong conclusions. One of the greatest pains the chronic critic can suffer is the pain of a new idea. The idea that personal power can be used constructively and effectively may be entirely beyond his comprehension. Remember, it is always easy to be the expert when you are not responsible for the results.

In England, there is a bill-collector whose specialty is getting payments from accounts that no one else has been successful with. He has his own technique: he soaks his coat in a foul-smelling substance, then goes in and hands the laggard a note with the amount due; he refuses to say anything, and soon is handed his money and ushered out the door. You can imagine the criticism this man enjoys!

Now I am not suggesting that you follow his example. It would probably make you sick. But the point being made is that this man gets the job done with utter disregard for his critics. You can use your power in more subtle ways, but with no more regard for critics than our odorous collector.

7. DON'T BE AFRAID TO USE YOUR PERSONAL COMMAND POWER

People with red hot command power can still be sensitive; they have no desire to trample the opposition unnecessarily. But they are not marshmallows, so frequently they must pursue their objectives despite opposition and criticism. Don't be afraid to use your PCP. True, you will ruffle a few feathers and hear a squawk now and then, but this will go away. However, if you back off in the misguided fear of disapproval, your power will suffer irreparable damage. Don't be afraid to use your command power: you will never lose anything of value by doing this.

Loren Cross, a commission salesman, respected his boss Alex Trimble and valued his good will. But, when Mr. Trimble approached Loren, insisting that he cut his commission in an effort to land a big account, Loren said no. Then Trimble complained that the company couldn't make any concessions, but that Loren certainly could and should, Loren still said no. When Trimble retorted that the cut Loren was asked to take was hardly enough to warrant friction and misunderstanding, Loren again said no. Finally, this man who wasn't afraid to use his command power to say no landed the order at regular prices and regular terms, and Loren's relationship with Mr. Trimble is now more solid than ever.

Don't be afraid to use your command power. Heat it up and use it when and where it will do the most good.

8. LIKE POWERFUL YOU

The most important player in the power game is you, and the most important opinion of that player is *yours*. You are the one who establishes your authority; you are the one who must decide when and where to use your power. Like yourself as a powerful person, since you can do much for yourself and the people around you. This is your right and your obligation.

9. A PROGRESS TEST

Now that you have explored the rewards and the risks of personal command power throughout this book, mull over the following progress test. You already have the techniques and methods of command power firmly in your grasp. This test is designed to be used as a double-check and to emphasize your attitude toward your power and its application. As every competent psychologist can tell you, your power will only be as great as you think it is. The alpha and the omega of all the power you will ever have lies between your ears.

If you answer "yes" to each of these questions, your power switch is on "go."

- Is your first loyalty to your own convictions?
- Are you willing to take risks?
- Do you enjoy a power image?
- Do you take your power responsibility seriously?
- Do you give yourself first claim on your power?
- Do you like the idea of motivating and controlling people?
- Do you place a high priority on personal achievement?
- Do you enjoy the challenge of being a leader?
- Can you bounce back after a temporary loss?
- Are you devoting your power to getting what you want?
- Can you stay organized and calm in the face of harassment?
- Do you refuse to feel guilty when others misunderstand and disapprove of you?
- Do you discount it when an opponent bad-mouths you?
- Do you brush envy and criticism aside?
- Do you consider yourself a constructive rebel?

- Do you have the self-image of a winner?
- Does it please you that you can also help others by winning?

This progress test is not meant to be used to grade or standardize you. That would be an affront to the singular power that lies within you. Instead, use it as a chart to keep your personal command power red hot!

INDEX